IN THE CENTER

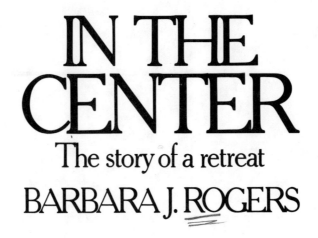

IN THE CENTER

The story of a retreat

BARBARA J. ROGERS

Ave Maria Press
Notre Dame, Indiana 46556

International Standard Book Number: 0-87793-266-2 (Cloth)

0-87793-267-0 (Paperback)

Library of Congress Catalog Card Number: 82-84468

Printed and bound in the United States of America.

Cover and text design: Elizabeth French

For Linda and Peter Sabbath

TABLE OF CONTENTS

ACKNOWLEDGMENTS

This book is based on the journals and autobiographical sketches written by the retreatants of the Thomas Merton Center for Contemplative Prayer, who generously gave me permission to quote them. I would like to thank Peter and Linda Sabbath, co-directors of the Center, for their encouragement of this project and contribution to it. They asked that their role in the retreat be minimized, but the reader should remember that without these two people the retreat would not have happened.

The Sabbaths have subsequently opened the St. Monica House of the Merton Center, 6423 Terrebone, in Montreal, and plan to open another center in the San Diego area.

Among others who have influenced this book, the following should be acknowledged: José de Vinck for his careful editing, Catherine de Vinck for her enthusiastic support, Jean Jack for her mothering, and Mark Gardner for being the friend he is.

BARBARA ROGERS

FOREWORD

Barbara Rogers has written the kind of book Thomas Merton would have liked. The book comes from a remarkable personal experience. She spent a month at the Thomas Merton Center for Contemplative Prayer. It was a month of self-analysis, intensive journal writing, meditation and prayer. Her significant book makes us a vital part of her journey.

The book is one Thomas Merton would have liked because the author's spirituality bears some resemblance to that of Merton. There is a great deal of personal candor in this book, a courageous willingness to deal with the self as it really is. Merton's honesty is one of the hallmarks of his spiritual life. His need to appreciate the real self rather than the empirical self which exists at the surface of our lives was a constant in his monastic years. Barbara Rogers, furthermore, manifests the same hesitations as Merton, about whether God has made much of a difference in her life. She seeks the realm of the sacred without surrendering the secular. Merton insisted that both go together.

In the Center reminded me of another, quite different writer. Graham Greene's *The End of the Affair* was the story of a woman who sought and found, lost and kept grace in the turbulence of human and divine love. The correlations with Greene are more remote than those with Merton but the hunger for God, the sense of personal unworthiness, the courage, the decision to let go of a deep friendship because of an assumed incompatibility with a deeper life of grace, the recording of all this in journal form, and the awareness of love through suffering and loss are all at the heart of Greene's story and Barbara Rogers' life.

She makes credible the longing for God that exists beneath the surface of so many contemporary lives. This longing is often disguised under another formality, e.g., the desire for a greater freedom, a comprehensive fidelity, a future which settles us, an acceptance which is total, true and personal. Barbara Rogers is critical in her assessments. She does not assume that those who speak easily of God are genuine. She wonders where God begins and where gimmicks or psychoses, fraud or obsession end. She has given us a series of splendid sketches, painfully intimate at times, of those on retreat with her. She has done this in a way that catches the heartache of a generation, the yearning for peace, the qualified but real personal victories people manage, the lack of sensitivity on the part of others which has scarred so indelibly the people who have come to the Center.

I found her book absorbing and enlightening. It was a privilege to read, an unforgettable story uniquely hers and yet somehow ours.

Anthony T. Padovano

INTRODUCTION

Writers are often the prophets who tell us what is happening in mankind at any given time in history. A recurrent modern theme among such prophets is alienation. Modern men and women have been thrust out from their secured place into an exile away from the known and familiar. Like a small boat slashed adrift by stormy winds and buffeted by a hostile ocean, moderns find themselves lost in an alienated world. None of us escapes this universal phenomenon.

If we are not physically alienated from our physical home, we are at least psychically and spiritually alienated as we struggle with our inner disintegration leading us into a terrifying, psychic angst. Spiritually we seem daily to be drifting farther away from a hidden God into a noisy, material world that makes his still voice almost impossible to hear.

Called to share intimacy

Yet when such darkness overcomes our personal universe, the dawn of a new enlightenment usually cannot be far away. The positive phenomenon we see unfolding within us and around us is a desire to experience an authentic love, deep intimacy between an *I-thou* in a *we* community.

From some prenatal source of knowledge we seem to know that God has created us to live in his ecstatic happiness and to find our identity as a unique, beautiful, free and loving person in the birth of the *I* that is begotten in the intimacy of a loving *we* community. We are searching desperately in every conversation, in every thought and action for another, who in intimate, loving oneness will birth us into our true being.

True Christianity is the revelation and the experience of the loving triune community of Father, Son and Holy Spirit that dwells within us. Such intimate presence is to be a continued growth in deepening faith, hope and love set like precious diamonds in the medium we call human consciousness.

Merton Center

About a dozen years ago Linda and Peter Sabbath established the Thomas Merton Center for Contemplative Prayer in Magog, Quebec, to offer a place for hungry pilgrims to deepen in inner silence the intimacy of God's indwelling, and to offer prayer-disciplines and techniques to aid in expanding human consciousness to become a fit medium for God's gifts.

This book is a story of the Merton Center as experienced by a group of people who recently spent a month under the guidance of Linda and Peter Sabbath.

The author most skillfully weaves together the personal histories of brokenness and healing of her and her fellow pilgrims as they strove to silence the noise in their hearts and listen in integrative, loving surrender to God's indwelling Word. She describes the various techniques used to "concentrate" or to move away from the illusory false self to become one with the true center, God.

She begins and ends by telling us her own journey and effortlessly shares the background and experiences of each of the other retreatants. We are vicariously led to experience in poignant and moving ways their death and resurrection experiences.

In the Center proves that real life and the stories of real people are more exciting than fiction. But this book is more and this is why I hope and pray many will read it. It is a story of what God's infinite love can do to heal all of us, whatever may be the skein of twisted, knotty threads that make up our own history. This book is a paean to God's humility, and that he loves us so much that he wishes to live intimately within us, to empty himself into our broken selves so we may be healed.

It is a story of what happened to a handful of modern Christians who went into the desert of their hearts but returned to share their healed selves in loving service with others.

It is the story, too, of what could happen to us if we only believed and acted on the Good News that God's intimate love, when deeply experienced in our brokenness, can heal us. And our healing will be measured by bringing God's love into the marketplace. May you experience what the author and her companions experienced. This is not only the story of your brokenness but your story of how you can be healed in the desert of your heart when you have the courage and discipline to confront God who burns with love from within you!

George A. Maloney, S.J.

IN A DRY SEASON

On the kitchen table
in a blue bowl
peaches with two active wasps.
The image enters the eye
then moves out, leaving
shadows, a residue of truth.

What I see, perceive as solid shapes
—chair, cupboard, stove—
are in fact tremulous masses
great hives of working atoms
assuming precarious forms.

How to stand squarely on the ground
knowing there are no hard limits:
what I touch is a trembling web
a frail structure giving way
tearing, torn beyond mending.

In a month of drought
time quivers, a water-drop
pushing itself slowly
out of the hose of summer;
not enough to wet the fingertips!
Yet, there it goes, rolling off
the curve of space, a single drop
compacted of ages and histories
falling without return
into the dark.

How to confront such world
of change, contradiction, loss?
It is enough to suddenly hear
rain slashing the window
it is enough to say
> Lord of the rainfall
> Lord of peaches and wasps
> Lord of my life
> Lord.

Catherine de Vinck, 1980

1 TOWARD THE CENTER

Yes, I am making a road
in the wilderness,
paths in the wilds.
                    Isaiah 43:19

"I hope you find what you're looking for," Martin said
to me at the overcrowded departure lounge of La Guardia
Airport.

He was staring over my head and down the hall, not at
me. His hands were clasped behind his back and his voice was
not very friendly. I had no right to expect it to be. Martin and
I had met only three months before, both divorced, wounded
and wary. A week later we had fallen in love, our defen-
siveness shaken by the surprise of finding another person
who not only could live with the accumulated crotchets of
our 45 years, but had the same ones. Sometimes we would
have to reach out and touch each other's faces, it was that
hard to believe what had happened to us.

"We belong to each other," Martin had said suddenly
one evening after a long silence, and it was true, we did. I had
never before felt I belonged to a man, and wouldn't have
liked it if I had. I wanted to belong to myself. That was one of
my problems.

"When I tell my parents," I said, worrying out loud, "my
father will ask, 'Is he rich?' (Martin was in debt.) My mother
will ask, 'Is he a Christian?' " (Martin is a non-practicing
Jew.) They would be dissatisfied with me, as usual.

"Tell them they forgot to ask the most important question." Martin smiled and his voice dropped to a dramatic
whisper. "Is he white?"

Our conversations always had a way of ending with

laughter. Kisses and laughter. I wanted him never to go home. Martin, whose memories of home were ugly ones, full of curses and violence, never wanted to go either.

Long before Martin and I fell in love, the arrangements had been made for my retreat at the Thomas Merton Center for Contemplative Prayer. Like many people who go to the Center, as I later learned, I had made such a mess of my life that only God could straighten it out. It was no good asking him to work miracles at critical moments, while you were losing your husband or your job or your mind. In a fit of self-pity you cry, "God help me. I'm sorry this time, really sorry." He must know that what you are really sorry about is that you haven't got what you wanted or you got it and didn't like it after all. Both were true of me. So I was on my way to a spiritual boot camp to learn how to let God take charge of my life. Some people came to the Merton Center on the verge of sanctity, some on the verge of suicide, but I wasn't in either category, just sad when I thought about my life, suspecting I was missing the whole point of it.

When Martin heard about my retreat, he couldn't believe it. His weather-beaten, freckled face was baffled. If I loved him, why was I leaving on this harebrained pilgrimage?

"A month of silence? Three hours of prayer every day?" Martin shook his head. "Get your money back."

He was a modern man, thoroughly suspicious of God, prayer and religious mania. They reminded him of the dark days before air-conditioning, throwaway bottles, and Ethical Culture, when people wore hair shirts and whipped themselves. He wanted no part of it. Maybe not of me either.

"Life is hard enough," Martin said as we waited in the airport departure lounge the day of my flight. "Why not just enjoy what comes along?" He paused, and one hand absently flattened his thick auburn hair where it rose high over his forehead. "You think God wants you to give me up because we're too happy? Is that it?"

I could only look at him, unable to answer, my arms circled loosely around his neck while he stood rigid and unaccommodating. Perhaps God expected me to give up any kind of human attachment, as the spiritual books call it. Apparently I couldn't love anyone without going into a security crisis, requiring round-the-clock devotion from some perfect lover. My attentions might better be confined to God, who presumably was up to them. Not knowing what was expected of me, I had no answer for Martin.

An automated voice announced over the loudspeaker that my Montreal flight was delayed for two hours, and Martin glanced at his watch. "I have appointments this afternoon. You'll have to wait by yourself."

At the time I thought he was being hard on me, but during the weeks at the Center, I began to understand his need to protect himself from being hurt by hurting first. I wasn't the only one who was afraid, though I tended to believe so.

"It's all right." My voice was carefully non-reproachful, though I already felt abandoned. I was practicing what I thought was detachment. "You go along." Actually I wanted him to forget about business, sit with me in the dim bar, hold my hand and give me some sign that he would still be there for me after the long month was over.

But he only patted my shoulder, gave me a quick good-bye kiss and was off, striding down the corridor, not looking back. He was leaving, not being left, choosing the more dignified alternative. Martin had troubles enough trying to hold his business together during the current recession. He was much too busy to compete with God.

"Competing was never my problem," I said to myself, 20,000 feet in the air, watching ranges of cloud-mountains shift and roll under the plane. All my life I believed people would love me if only I did great things. "Perform, perform!" they said, clapping the way a crowd does when trying to coax a would-be suicide to jump out of a skyscraper window.

Like many modern women, I had altogether embraced

the active life, cutting a swath in the world with single-minded violence, grimly reaping. I valued what men valued and was determined to have it, just like my hard-driving, hedonistic, Madison Avenue father. The contemplative path is seldom chosen in our culture, perhaps because we mistake receptivity for weakness, although Jesus had said to Martha, "Mary has chosen the better part," glad of her silent attention as she sat listening at his feet. Despite these words, I continued to play the part that brought me recognition and power, not the one that might bring me peace. At 20 I had choreographed the accomplishments of my life as neatly as a one-woman *Swan Lake*. Not a step was missed, but the curtain never seemed to come down, and I could never rest.

Only with Martin had I caught a glimpse of what it was like to be loved for no reason at all. No good works, no performances. If I cried, he comforted me. If I wanted to dance or sing, he did it with me, both of us silly and wild as kids. His presence in my life had been a healing one. Thinking about Martin wouldn't do, I told myself. The trip to Canada was supposed to cure me of looking before and after. "Consider the lilies of the field," Jesus said. "They toil not, neither do they spin. Yet I say to you, not Solomon in all his glory was arrayed like one of these." Nevertheless, I toiled and spun and worried. I was worried now, as we were circling over Montreal, not at all sure I, a long-time workaholic, would make it as a lily of the field.

In our Western culture the search for God is considered so quaint that when I got off the plane, the customs officer gave me a suspicious second look on hearing the purpose of my journey—a month-long religious retreat. Yet what I was attempting was neither new nor strange. Always, in every religious tradition, it had been known that seeing God meant seeing nothing else. All outward stimuli must be quieted, all attention concentrated on melting away the barriers we have built to shelter our egos, to protect our fragile, fearful selves, and to gather what we can of this world's goods. For a long time I had every good the world could offer, and I had protected my ego so thoroughly that it sat enthroned somewhere in my head, fat and smug as a maharajah. The Center's brochure offered another kind of good, another kind of living, but I was unsure that either existed outside TV commercials and self-help books.

When the French-speaking taxi driver left me at the entrance to the Center, I stood at the door for a long while, trying to decide whether or not to go in. The farmhouse is close to a little road that leads up the side of the lake from the town of Magog. On either side of the old building are additions: the bright, rustic two-story annex in which the Sabbath family lives, and the new unfinished Chapel of the Transfiguration, a modern, light-filled little structure with a huge bay window bringing the meadow, mountain and sky into the undecorated room. A graceful Louis Quinze table, its legs curving over a small Oriental rug, served as altar. Above it a brass bird, its wings swept back till they touched at the tips, held the host during the adoration in the evenings. No statue or stained glass distracted the eye; only the Bible on its tall stand and flowers arranged on the floor furnished the stark emptiness of the chapel. It was a model for the emptiness we were to encourage in ourselves.

The Center had been founded 10 years before, and hundreds of people had already gone through its training program. At least 90 percent of them got what they had come for, or so the brochure claimed. Montreal's archbishop had recognized the value of Linda and Peter Sabbath's work by inviting them to set up a training center in the city, where adults could absorb on weekends what retreatants learned by immersion in the solitude and silence of the farm 80 miles away. But when Linda first began the Center, no one knew who she was. To her neighbors, she was only a sturdy, handsome woman with long, heavy brown hair, twinkling brown eyes pushed up at the outside corners by high cheekbones and a bright, sudden smile that made her face look as it had in her

youth, when she had been a model, much sought after by
men.

Until her thirties, Linda had been an atheist like her
Ukrainian immigrant father, whose brutality had taught her
first to rebel and in the end to forgive. Her study with the
great Japanese Zen master, Yasutani Roshi, gave her a first
glimpse of the interior life, but she ultimately felt more need
for divine love than Zen could fill in her. She had first gone to
Yasutani Roshi as a favor to Thomas Merton, who was not
allowed to leave his Trappist monastery at the time. In this
instance as in others, his young Canadian friend served as a
sensitive barometer to the experiments in contemplation
springing up across North America. Just before Merton's sudden death in Bangkok in 1968, he and she had been preparing
to found a meditation community for contemplatives of all
traditions. Merton was planning to make contact with
Eastern monks and nuns who might join such a community,
but the idea did not survive him. After he died, Linda decided
to leave her work in religious studies at McGill University
and live as she felt God was calling her to live, in Christian
community.

The Center began as a ramshackle farmhouse and barn
with 125 rolling acres in the eastern townships of Quebec. For
a woman who later said that her most strenuous effort in the
past had been to lift a cocktail glass, the shock of farm life
was a hard one. An architect, looking at the old house, shook
his head and told her, "Better burn it down." Like her other
friends from the city, who came out briefly and departed
with condolences, the architect thought her house and her
plans hopeless. Linda felt no great loss when winter settled in
that first year and her friends stayed home before their cozy
Montreal fireplaces, no longer reminding her of the farmhouse's defects.

In time the hand-hewn beams, stone fireplace and wide-
plank floors were revealed, but when Linda moved in, the
family had to walk around a gaping hole in the floor through

which one could see the rough stone cellar. The place was filthy because animals had lived in it alongside the poor squatters who were hardly cleaner than their beasts. There was no heat. Water from a garden hose had to be used to break up the dirt caked on the living-room floor. Linda and her children spent the winter bundled into snowmobile suits, gathering wood for fires and huddling around the hearth, waiting to go to bed where their own body heat might keep them warm.

How a woman alone could face such a Siberian exile, I had trouble understanding. Just the thought of repairing my sprawling Tudor house in New Jersey, once I was divorced and on my own, sent me into a fetal position under the bedclothes. Martin had rescued me and my house, building storm windows, wrapping little jackets around the pipes in the basement to insulate them. "They feel warm," he said, which by some law of paradox I still can't grasp, indicates that they want jackets. Over the weeks he had reconstructed my house and me, patient as an archeologist restoring the tombs of the Ptolemies. "I like to fix things," was all he said when I thanked him. "Broken things make me sad." Broken people made Martin feel sad too, but he felt he couldn't help them because they needed more love than he could give. Yet the love he gave me was always enough, and when I heard Linda's story of six years in the wilderness without a man to turn to for help and love, I wondered at her strength. Her children too apparently wondered at this mother of theirs who was so different from everyone else's. I came to know only one of these children, the oldest, a large, stunning woman, strong-willed, witty, mocking Peter and Linda with a mix of resentment and love, working like a serf as cook for their retreats, even while she mocked.

Linda watched her children's embarrassment at their poverty, pride in their differentness and first hesitant steps toward spiritual lives of their own, wondering if she had given them a stone instead of bread. Other women, she knew, were raising their children with the help of Dr. Spock, but his book had nothing in it about how to bring up children in a monastery. All three were jealous of the time Linda spent with retreatants; the retreatants were jealous of the time she spent with her children. In speaking of those hard years, Linda seems surprised at sympathy, saying they were full of joy, not pain. As she told her son when he was humiliated by being poor, "There's no sacrifice if you're in love."

In going to Magog, Linda realized that in the world's eyes she had done a crazy thing by resolving to let others know Jesus was theirs for the touching. She had been touched by him and knew that no words, no doctrine, no institution and no book could take the place of the experience that had sent her into the wilderness.

Sometime before, she had been in contact with the Christian poet Catherine de Vinck, an earthy, laughing mother of six children, now grandmother of six more. Catherine had in her poetry and letters poured into the mold of words what Linda had felt in her wordless prayer. What Catherine wrote after tending one helpless, forever-infant son and five other children made Linda surer of what she must do to bring the Center to life. She must show those who came there that contemplation goes on not only in the chapel, but throughout the ordinary day's work. At this writing Linda and Catherine have never met, but they have done their best to mend all the broken children sent to them, and sometimes traded them back and forth.

I was one of those children. When I arrived at the Center, knowing I was in someone else's hands as soon as I walked in, Linda, the tidy housekeeper, snatched up me and my messes, knowing with St. Paul that if one part of the body suffers, all the other parts suffer with it. "Whoever walks through that door," she told me later, "I have a physical feeling for, almost a pain. You were the one I was going to guide personally, though Peter had wanted me to do nothing because I had been sick and needed rest." Peter is her husband, much younger, a man drawn to the Center and converted there, not leaving his Judaic heritage but filling it full. His face is weather-beaten like Martin's and looks older than his real age. A short, curly brown beard gives him the roughhewn appearance of the *sabras* I knew in Israel, born and brought up on the rocky, unrewarding land they worked. Over his frequent mild half-smile presides a long curved nose, sensitive as an animal's. At the beginning it was the animals that attached him to the Center, for with them he could be silent, yet not alone.

Peter had been the first permanent resident of the Center. In the early days, he was neither Jew nor Christian, but a seeker after the unknown God, who might be one final illusion in a path littered with illusions. Because Peter could see the emptiness lying at the end of every lifework but the service of God, he had been unable to settle for any career, either in business or in the concert world as the pianist he might have become. So he wandered across Canada and the United States, hitchhiking with his dog, practicing a little yoga, a little Zen, waiting for a teacher to happen to him, and planning vaguely to wind up as some kind of monk. Which kind he had no idea. In Linda, who had meanwhile been waiting for the man who would direct the Center, Peter found the teacher he was seeking. Later, after their marriage, he became her teacher as much as she had been his. But at first he had been only an intense, quiet young man with wild long hair, big, shining blue eyes and no spiritual roots, even in his own Jewish tradition, a rebel and apparent atheist who devoured the writings of St. Teresa of Avila. For the first year he worked on the farm while genuine and would-be contemplatives came and went. Through the procession of the seasons, the feeding of animals and being a father to Linda's children, Peter became a Christian, Linda's husband and co-director of the Center. Linda let him lead, with a tired gladness, saying to everybody, "This is Peter's office. No one can go in, not even me, unless we ask first." It was Peter who led us through the retreat. Linda rested and watched the children come, keeping still.

At that time, the Center was one of the many loosely structured contemplative communities in North America. People who wanted a place to pray and be still visited in greater and greater numbers, and soon Peter and Linda themselves were too busy for contemplation. With Peter's help, Linda was able to organize retreats in alternate months, leaving the residents some time for their own souls to breathe. The first formal retreatants arrived during the spring rains, when the grounds were turned to mud, the cesspool had overflowed and the only toilet had backed up. Three visiting nuns, used to the privacy, comfort and spotlessness of their Michigan convent, lasted a week and then went home, kindly telling Linda and Peter, "The Lord told us to leave." Despite the austerity of life at the old farmhouse, other retreatants came and stayed, passing the word that this broken-down place was full of God. Pooling their labors, they rebuilt the house into the historic landmark it is today. Over the years Peter shared the work of direction with Linda, but by the time I came, directing us was almost entirely his job.

Peter seemed to know our minds better than we did, perhaps because he too had once been a retreatant here. When on that first day all of us gathered around the indoor picnic table for our first meeting, Peter began the work of making this houseful of strangers into a family. He sat at the head of the table like a serious father. After telling us what we could expect during our month of silence, work and wordless prayer, he asked, "Why are you here?" his face open and ready to be amazed by whatever we said. The answers came, frankly and without fear.

Jane, a brilliant, intense woman in her late thirties, gripped her fingers and said she could not rest until God had touched her to her depths. Later she chose the filthiest part of the barn to clean because she wanted more than anything to be clean herself, before God. Jane also chose not to tell her story for this book because God, whom she had once approached through clever words and good behavior, had now become too much to be spoken of. In the end the retreat did its work on her, and she heard "things which cannot be put into words, things which human lips may not speak."

Therese, a golden-haired young housewife, sat next to her, saying that she was there to know Jesus, to put him in the place where the world now stood in her life. A heavy-set Christian Brother, Jonathan, said that he wanted to become for others what Jesus was for him but that he had a long way to go. Brother Jonathan laughed, spreading his hands. "Look at me: hardly molded in the image of God!"

Beside him sat Michael, a man in his late seventies who kept his hands tightly folded. "I've always wanted to know the Lord," he said. "Only that."

"To know him and love him," said Robert, the tall, strikingly handsome young man in the next seat. "That's what I want." He paused and looked down at his hands, blushing. "Always have. Since I was a little kid. But something gets in the way." That same day I overheard this beautiful bearded giant say to another retreatant, "I'm having trouble with my sexuality," and wondered how such a smiling, perfect man could have any such trouble. Later, I learned that he was a seminarian and had found the rule of celibacy impossible to keep. He looked around quickly at the women in the room, then at the pencil he kept twirling between his long, thick fingers.

Anna, a nun of 40, sat next to him, straight and still. "The past troubles me," she said, a charming French Canadian lilt to her low voice. "God is not present to me as I would wish." She bowed her head.

Paul, a blond, husky young priest, who had been a missionary in Brazil, spoke from his place by the screen door, where he kept glancing out at the forested hill across the road. "I was lost down there," he said, clearly struggling not to say too much, letting his quick, flying hands speak for him until he remembered to hold them still. "Nobody had time to pray. Neither did I. If I don't pray, something goes wrong."

Alison, a tall, dark-haired writer, fidgeted with her napkin. "I'm not sure it can be done," she said finally, "but I'd hoped to find God here. Now I don't know."

In the silence that followed Alison's not knowing, we all sat looking at the table, not at each other, for as yet we felt no closeness. Sister Anna's teaspoon fell to the floor and she bumped her head against stout Brother Jonathan's when they both tried to pick it up. We were like children at a dancing lesson, wanting to make the right move, but embarrassed. Peter took us up, not afraid of the mistakes we would make.

"Tomorrow you'll start practicing your breath prayer," he said. "It doesn't have to be the Jesus Prayer, the one asking God to have mercy on you, but if you want that prayer, say it. The idea is to find the words that say what you want to be. That could change over the weeks, but right now, what prayer do you want to be? I don't mean say, I mean *be*. That's what the breath prayer is, something you become, take into yourself. It's not a 'vain repetition.' Don't be afraid that's what it is. As you breathe in and out, you let this short breath prayer become you. Let it tell God what your love is, then be that love. Say it when you get up, work, go to sleep. Tape it on your hand, your rake, your place at the table. Be this prayer and let it be you." Peter always ended by looking around the table at each one of us as if trying to detect and answer unspoken questions from the shy ones. I was not one of those, but said nothing, for once in my life.

Before going to the Center, however, I had never tried praying without many words. To give up words seemed to be giving up myself. My prayers were set pieces, like something to be delivered over a P.A. system. Instead of listening, I was merely babbling to God.

I was embarrassed by the idea of having nothing to say

but a childish phrase over and over again, as Peter was telling us to do, and imagined how boring it would be. From his place at the head of the table, Peter smiled at us, as if he knew what we were thinking, but also knew that God was never bored. He told us to take a break. We all went outside, and I stood behind the fir trees Linda had planted to shield her children from curiosity seekers.

When I came back to the picnic table in the front room of the farmhouse, Peter was telling a little story about the mystical life, perhaps trying to make the whole enterprise seem less exotic, more ordinary. Alison was writing it down so furiously that the point of her pencil kept tearing through the paper, while she chewed the corners of her lower lip. Peter's story was intended to help us understand what we were doing at the Center, in case we didn't know.

"Once there was a fish swimming around in the ocean," he said. "The fish wondered about this sea he'd heard of and decided to go and ask the Queen Fish what was going on. She was supposed to know, being a queen. So he went and asked her. 'I've heard of the sea,' he said, swimming back and forth before the throne. 'What is this sea?' The queen, probably thinking something was the matter with this particular fish, but understanding that he hadn't been awake till now, said, 'Why you're in it. The sea is what you live, move and have your being in.' "

Blond Therese, the pretty housewife from Ontario, sat listening like a child, her mouth a little open. "Yes!" she said aloud, having forgotten us all. Then she put her hands over her cheeks and looked down, probably hoping we hadn't heard her.

After telling his story, Peter was silent awhile. "God is the sea we swim in," he said finally. "I guess you know that or you wouldn't be here. But you have to know it really, not just think it or have faith in it the way you have faith in words from a book. When you read and say, 'In him we live and move and have our being,' you need to keep those words in your hands while you work. And you will work here, only as much as you feel is right for you." He half-glanced at old Michael, who had recently suffered a heart attack. Michael seemed to understand he was being let off the hook and started to protest. Then he smiled, kept quiet and put a finger against his lips as if he were warning himself.

"Physical work," Peter went on, "is how you practice carrying your prayer into the world, being God's hands. Use the breath prayer and let it work in you." His words reminded me of the letter I'd received from the Center about austerity and inconvenience. The Center was no resort, and everybody had to clean up after himself, sometimes after others.

"I'm going to be bad at this," I thought, knowing how I hated manual labor, cursed it every time I had to leave my books for it. The $700 this adventure was costing me might have paid for a month in a cottage by the sea, writing and dreaming, lying on the sand next to Martin who loved the sea as I did. Pulling myself up against the dream, I stopped thinking of what was not and tried to be a lily of the field, living in the moment as Martin always did.

A beginning would have to be made. At least I could weed and clean and say my breath prayer, not looking ahead. Just day by day I would do it and time would pass.

As it passed, I punctuated the days with entries in my journal. We all wrote journals, so the Center staff could see at a glance where we were. After every prayer session and work period, we would write a few words. It used to irritate me the way Alison, Jane and Brother Jonathan would rush out of the chapel, grab their journals and start scribbling. They no doubt had something remarkable to tell, I thought, wishing for something too. It never occurred to me to make up an experience. On this retreat I was going to be completely honest for once in my life. No self-delusion or deluding of others. If something miraculous happened to me, very well, but I was not going to be enthused into saying it had when it hadn't. So I watched these carried-away people run for their notebooks, feeling a pang of envy, a stiffening of resolve.

Especially I envied beautiful Therese, rich, married, a young mother and coming close to God in her youth, not wasting it as I had. If I had known her story, how close she had been to taking her own life, I would not have envied her. But at the time I knew nothing except that I wanted to be at home, close to Martin, close to someone who made me feel loved. That night began a month-long series of bad dreams. The quiet focusing on my breath prayer all day and the atmosphere of security and freedom from responsibility released every demon in my unconscious. I awoke, cried and fell asleep again half a dozen times every night.

In one dream, early in the retreat, my daughter and I escaped from the violence of war into a Byzantine church, where Martin's face loomed large and benevolent like the place's patron saint. A week afterward, Martin appeared in another dream, this time cold, distant and uncaring. I awoke, sure that he no longer loved me as he had before, sure that he was with someone else. Later Martin told me that he had spent that night, July 10, with another woman. He was lonely and figured I was only a flash in the pan. The other woman seemed more real. A healing process was going on during this midnight scenario of mine, but at the time it felt like a sickness.

None of these things appeared in my journal, nor were they called for. We were supposed to write brief entries about each of our practices, though Alison, being a writer, spent hours at her journal, still working at the dining room table when the rest of us were going upstairs to bed. Peter had us gaze at a brown paper square with a gold circle in the middle, trying to clear our minds of all thoughts or words. For me, it was this particular practice which ultimately proved most valuable, but in the beginning it seemed like the gimmicks teachers used on me in Sunday school to keep me quiet while my mother was in church.

If we were able to use our breath prayer while we worked, or if the work seemed dry and hard, we were to say so in our journals. No exalted ramblings or psychological analyses were encouraged. Brother Jonathan had sighed when told not to run on in his journal and declared that a great talent was going to waste if he were not allowed to ramble in public. Alison chewed her lip and went on writing in her spiral notebook, like a recording angel. What the journal was for, though, was not self-expression or release, but simply to give the staff a record of our state of mind. They didn't want us to bare our souls, just to give warning if we were getting crazy.

Actually, Peter told us, only one person out of the hundreds who had come, ever went over the edge and that one didn't fall far. He left in the middle of the month, scared of what he might be getting into. Some people weren't ready to face themselves before God, and I understood how they felt, being none too ready myself, expecting to be scorched by the burning bush. If it became too much to be as naked as silence and solitude would make us, we should say so and get the help we needed. Old Michael was being monitored for his heart condition, I later learned, and Sister Anna for her depression. I remembered that the initial brochure from the Center had specified that no one should come there who was inexperienced in prayer, under psychiatric care or merely curious. At the time, I assumed they were warning off people like me, who were not saints. But worries about my inadequacy were not enough to turn me away from what the Sabbaths had to offer. Always before I had come through when something was asked of me. Sure, I would cry alone in the laundry, dissolve in the middle of the night when everyone else was asleep, but I figured I was at least normal. Whatever these other people, near-saints or not, could do, so could I.

Besides, I thought with a certain pride, they were mostly priests and nuns who came here. Someone had always taken care of their material needs. They didn't know how hard life was in the real world where no one takes care of you. Because I knew, I had an advantage. That it was necessary for me to have an advantage should have been a warning in itself, but if it was, I ignored it, as I had ignored warnings all my life.

The breath prayer felt good to me. I could ask for help without anyone seeing me do it, admit how deep the old sadness went, how unparented I felt even in the presence of God the Father. Walking around the Center's grounds, watching the grass bend under my feet, I wanted to start my life over, but didn't know how, not realizing the work had already begun. The breath prayer was a knowledge in itself, and as it turned out, the discipline of taking one thing at a time was right for me. All my life I had resisted the life-pattern of my gentle, merry, slow-moving Southern mother, who could spend all day at a single task. As I left for school in the morning, she would start to clean out a dresser. She would still be at it when I came home. "Look what I found," she would beam at me. "Your great-grandmother's diary. She wrote it in Italy, during her tour, when she was 15 like you." All the women in my mother's family took the grand tour, and when they came home, they married and lived for their men.

My mother, though stubborn occasionally and a rebel against housework, was able to sacrifice herself in her turn. She suffered through chronic illness, my father's drunkenness, my brother's near-crippling polio and 20 years of teaching spoiled suburban second-graders with her good humor and faith in God still alive and well, the better for rough trials, like good metal under fire. All these small, dark-haired, blue-eyed women stood behind me, strong, humble, loving God fiercely and single-mindedly as cloistered nuns with no one else to love. They were good, holy women, these ancestors of mine, not hard and self-centered like their men, whom I more resembled than I did them. My own daughter is of the same tribe as all the grandmothers; love drives her as it drives the sun and other stars. She will sacrifice herself in her turn. But somehow the chain broke with me, its weakest link.

Like my father I am big, blond, self-willed, wanting to be fed more than to feed, always demanding more of the moment than it can reasonably give, squeezing the people around me until they hardly know if it's their love I want or their death. I watch other women smilingly defer to the whims of husbands, but with wonder and wrath, unable to follow their way. For my female ancestors, being what they were was enough. The tasks that filled their days were carried off the way primitive women hoed the corn or beat wet clothes on rocks, with friendly talk and songs. They were satisfied with what they were and what they had. If they could have seen me, late at night over my books, grim as a fury, my mind filled with a number of things, they would not have recognized me as one of them. They took a day at a time as infants take steps, with their minds on their business and nowhere else.

I had never been able to sacrifice my life to the people around me, or give myself to whatever moment I was in. And I feel the weight of my heroic female ancestors the way the pope must feel the burden of apostolic succession. During my time at the Center, the weight was lifted by the breath prayer, which required no performance, only attention. The breath prayer reminded me that I had only to concentrate, putting one foot before the other, one moment behind the next, in a single, unbroken stride.

We began to understand why we needed no reading, no television, no drinks, no cigarettes. All the old distractions were dissolved in the immediate, breathed words that set us humming like a hive full of bees ready for flight, ready for honey from flowers, hungry. Without the breath prayer, our prayers in the chapel would have been shouted into the wind. What we repeated as we walked, worked and ate was a Word that had made the world and us. We said it over and over, knowing that in the beginning was the Word and that the Word was with God and the Word was in fact God, dwelling among us, near and familiar as air.

Some of the retreatants never got much beyond the breath prayer, but were satisfied anyway that they had been filled to the brim. Alison, the writer of books, was one of these. I watched her move nervously around the farmhouse, her hands perpetually busy, as if they missed some compulsive occupation. Cigarettes, probably, I thought, as Alison bit her nails, chewed the end of her pencil and sighed frequently. The retreat was clearly hard going for Alison and generous souls like stout Brother Jonathan and skinny old Michael went out of their way to smile at her.

2 THE STORY OF ALISON

Trust in the Lord with all your heart. Never
rely on what you think you know. Remember
the Lord in everything you do, and he will
show you the right way. Never let yourself
think that you are wiser than you are; simply
obey the Lord.

Proverbs 3:5-7

Until Peter mentioned the journal, Alison had been feeling discouraged, sure that she could never sit still three hours
a day and keep quiet all day long. Ten years as an author-
lecturer had trained her in perpetual motion, for which she
got high pay and sometimes even love. Those years had also
brought her to the edge of a breakdown. Now she sat biting
the skin around her ragged nails, glad at least to be writing a
journal that would be read and appreciated by those in
charge of this mysterious place. And yet she wondered if the
journal would be no more than another performance,
another dramatized self trotted out to be admired. At night
she often dreamed of being a dancer, on the stage before an
audience of thousands, leaping to impossible heights, spinning, hanging in midair. All her life, midair was where she
had hung.

Whatever she did became something she couldn't enjoy,
and longed to be free of. While she raised children, she imagined herself a writer. Later as a writer, she imagined herself
a simple wife, loved by a man, bearing his child. It was not
too late for that, Alison knew, aware of her still-good body
and pretty face. Somebody worth having might still want
her, as had Jack, the lover she had taken after her divorce.
She had come to Canada to get away from whatever it was
Jack had done to her, not to think about it anymore. But he

was still sitting in her mind like a toad, looking ugly, though he had once seemed to her as beautiful as God. Her father sat there too, and sometimes the two blurred in her sight, becoming an audience of one, the audience that gave nothing back.

A psychiatrist had told her, during three months of therapy after the divorce, that her real audience was her father, who had never paid much attention to her or anyone else. And here she was, still thinking deep down that good works would buy his love, and the world's. Perhaps she even believed that God's love would be won that way. Alison did not want to believe she was on retreat to perform for God, but it might be true. She had been through enough therapy to know why she couldn't live in the real moment, only in the past or the future or some imaginary mock-up of both. "Whatever it is you have," said the therapist, who was very taken by her, a reaction Alison worked hard to produce, "you want something else. You need to concentrate on *now*, on what you really have."

What the therapist failed to see, Alison said to her friends, when they sat around talking about their therapists' defects, was that by all rights she should be happy and wasn't. She was good-looking, healthy, enjoyed her work, made money at it, got love when she wanted it. She was a success, as everyone always said she would be, but why, she asked the admiring therapist, did she always feel as if her hands and mouth were full of dust?

"I never liked what I really have," Alison objected, sure in her own mind she had no reason to like the long nights in a tiny apartment with croupy babies, or the company dinners that took three days of peeling, chopping and marinating to prepare, or gathering the dust that rolled like tumbleweed under the beds. Once she had done it to please God, for she had been converted at 21, sure that she would become another St. Teresa of Avila or at least a stigmatic. For some time after her conversion, she actually felt pains in her palms and wondered if they were holy pains. She was self-conscious about her daily Masses, her long prayers, her palm-pains and thought she was headed for great things. In the meantime, she endured the dirty diapers, the squabbles, the meals that had to be shoveled down the eternally open mouths of these eternally present children who left marshmallow stains and wrinkles where they gripped the legs of her slacks. "Someday I'll get out of this," she used to say to herself. "Meanwhile I'll pretend I'm someplace else."

So in her head she was for all those years a dancer, a skater, a writer, a separate self, unrelated to those marshmallow-handed, noisy, wanting little people. "Someday they will be gone," she thought for years. "Someday I will be myself, not them." All the while she knew the good days were slipping by, uncelebrated. Little Suzy sat beside her, patted her face and seemed to understand she was heavy and still with morning sickness. Asking for nothing, Suzy touched her mother's face with fingers light as wings. Three-year-old Jamie, the clumsy one who later became an athlete, fell down on the floor, saying apologetically, "I forgot to stand up." Instead of laughing, Alison thought he probably had brain damage. "I will spend all my life taking care of this strange child with his damaged brain," she thought. "God, why did you give me these children? I don't know who they are." The children grew between her arms, under her eyes, away from her, and Alison feared and sighed, wishing God had anesthetized her during all those ordinary days and years, only waking her up for the peak moments.

Maybe Peter's breath prayer was what she should have had all along, Alison thought, conscious of the hard picnic bench and the space between her fingers where she longed to hold a cigarette. She looked around her at handsome Robert's glistening, ruddy face and looked away when he stared back at her. Therese, she noticed, sat forward on her chair listening to Peter talk about the breath prayer, her mouth open like a starved child's. How could anyone be so eager for God, Alison wondered. One would think she had nothing else to live for, but as Alison knew, Therese had only joy in her life, only love. Lucky girl, she thought bitterly. No wonder she's so grateful to God. No wonder she loves the way she does.

Alison cupped her hands over her eyes and yawned, tired of hearing about the breath prayer and how it must be prayed every moment of her life. She would rather have read Peter's words in a book and distanced them by the reading. Anything was better than the hour she was living in, if living was the word for what she did. Alison stared at the beamed ceiling and parted her long dark hair with spread fingers. Once she had imagined doing whatever she did for God. Now she had no idea how to go about letting moments happen to her in his time rather than her own. She was in charge and wanted to be. Alison had left home and a strict father in her late teens, determined never again to let anyone run her life.

When Jerry, her gentle, stubbornly old-fashioned husband had wanted her to "stay a little girl," as he put it, and let him take care of her, Alison got angry and distant. "He doesn't want a woman," she thought and let him gradually drift away after 20 years of marriage to find himself the little girl he wanted, who had never been successful at anything except stealing Alison's husband. Alison was furious at him, furious at God. "I've worked so hard and never enjoyed a single moment of my life," she said in a sort of prayer, "and now you pay me back like this." She stopped going to church, figuring that would show God how mad at him she was.

During this time in her life when she felt particularly unloved, a brilliant, 24-year-old poet fell in love with her and wound up trying to kill himself in a bid for attention. Alison had been intoxicated by the notion that someone loved her enough to think of her night and day, as the young poet claimed he did, and to regulate his life by her comings and goings as if she were the sun. The tall, skinny boy, with his thick spectacles, hung about staring at her miserably, writing her poems so good they shamed her vanity. Of course she believed he was in love, because she wanted to believe it. As it turned out, he was only a poor schizophrenic, trying to plug himself into what others had led him to believe was the real world. His love was no more than the blind urge a bee has to find its hive. Alison had read that the lovemaking of insects, as of humans, can take strange forms. Flies caught in a flood of chemical desire attempt to mate with raisins. While Alison had imagined herself an Isolde, sought like the Holy Grail for her exquisite qualities, she was only a raisin after all. After the boy's suicide attempt, he was given electric shock treatments which made him forget all about Alison. She was sorry for him a little, but annoyed that a few volts of electricity was all it took to make someone stop loving her.

The short-circuited passion of the young poet should have warned Alison that she could expect nothing from the sort of love she had in mind, but she learned hard. It took an affair with another sort of young man, out to take whatever he wanted from the world, to cure Alison of her craving for romantic love. Young Jack was a Christian of sorts, floundering in his faith because it conflicted with his egotism, not happy with the wife he had chosen seven years before for her good looks and virtuous opinions. She had drawn him to Christianity and he had put himself under its yoke, without finding the burden easy or light. He wanted a perfect woman and expected to have one, because he believed he was perfect himself. Actually he was, by the world's measure—a war veteran, tall, blondly handsome, intelligent, wealthy, given to poetry and art when he wasn't racing his yacht.

Alison knew what she was doing when she began the affair. The ordinary life of writing, lecturing and looking out for Benjamin, her 16-year-old, had become as dry and boring as ordinary life had always been. Even God was boring to her and she no longer tried to pray. What she wanted was the certainty that she was put first, that she was wonderful and loved.

For a while Jack played his part, liking to hear that he too was wonderful. He wrote her awkward little poems, brought her flowers, told her he hated his wife and wished her dead. Alison sat across the table from him in their favorite tavern and listened gladly. Sometimes Jack talked about how he feared and felt the presence of the devil. He got her to keep the Ouija board, which his wife had ordered out of their apartment, at her house. Jack talked about the devil and how he would like the devil's kind of power, while Alison began to wonder if they had a Christian friendship after all. In time the friendship became an altogether physical one. They both wanted to believe they were special, beyond whatever rules God had set up for ordinary people.

In time, too, they began to hate each other. Jack hated Alison because she was not the perfect woman he thought would be worthy of him. She hated Jack because he had told her lies about planning to leave his wife. They never talked anymore of his hope to become a minister or of hers to become a teacher of the poor. They had come to live in a world where nothing was real to them but their shared delusions, which finally melted in the sunlight of real life, always Alison's enemy. Jack returned to his wife and business, leaving Alison all by herself to imagine whatever she wanted to. But Alison was tired of imagining her life instead of living it, of making up gods to believe in. Jack had been a god for her, and she had found him a poor, small god. When he left her, she was empty, with no delusions left. It was not the worst place to be, she had learned on coming to the Center. The grain of wheat had to die if anything were to come of it. She would put herself in God's hands, bury herself in the common earth of every moment, for they were the same thing. After all she had done and failed to do, she would say with St. Paul, "The one who plants and the one who waters really does not matter. It is God who matters because he makes the plant grow."

The past was something Alison had always wanted to

forget and rooting herself in each moment might be the way.
For her, the present moment had always been like a sick
stomach full of bad food from the day before. She had not
known until now that there might be a cure for what ailed
her. The past could not take her over if the present filled her
full. When Peter talked about the breath prayer, Alison
decided to use the ancient one of the Greek Christians, "Lord
Jesus Christ, have mercy on me, a sinner." That sounded
right to her. She was certainly a sinner, certainly in need of
whatever fixing she could get.

Linda sat down with her at the end of Peter's talk, looking large and still as a boulder, and told her that maybe this
wasn't the right prayer. "What would you have said as a
child?" she asked. "What would your words have been for
the thing you needed most?"

"I don't know," Alison answered, embarrassed because
of the child she still was. "Maybe hurt, sore. Maybe insides,
because that's where the hurt seemed to stick. That was my
word for the place."

"All right," Linda said, writing in the journal. "Why not?
'Lord heal my sore insides.' Would that say it?" She raised her
eyebrows, not saying anything more, not expecting anything
from Alison, just being available.

"Sure," Alison told her, glad Linda had thought her
child-self worth resurrecting. "I'd better start at the beginning." After that, she began saying the words of the breath
prayer to herself, walking around slowly, forgetting what it
was to be a grown-up, to read books, to think about important things.

Alison wondered how she would live with the breath
prayer which anchored her firmly and constantly in the present, but found to her relief that it blotted out the past, the
future, her father, all that was not itself. But the violent past
erupted in dreams, like the one in which she was again with
Jack, offering him a rich meal which he refused. Then he
stood by watching while two of his friends beat her up. It was

not until then that she noticed how much he looked like her father. Another night she dreamed she was in a ratty little hotel room, trying to sleep, when a small, determined girl broke in, asking for her parents. Alison knew the parents were dead and felt a great sorrow for the little girl. Now the child would have to start over, not looking back.

The evening after she had had the dream of being beaten up, Alison found that the past might be changed after all. She sat before her gold circle taped against the wall in front of her, gazing as she had been told to do, at a dark circle ringed with light, until her eyes watered from exhaustion and tears. Something she described in her journal as the sun in almost total eclipse became a burning pain in the top of her brain and traveled through her body. "Poor old man," she said to herself, suddenly thinking of her sick, tired father, sunk in his alcoholism and failures. "Poor old man." It seemed to her she was not so much the forgiver as the very act of forgiveness. She and her father exchanged places for the long moment of the pain, and she felt the poverty of his Ozark childhood and his humiliation at being barefoot in winter. The bell rang, signalling the end of the meditation hour just as Alison's tears began to fall for her father and herself. She hardly knew the difference between the two, but she was certain the light ringing the golden circle on the wall was about to burst around her and pull her into itself, like a rock circling a star in a failing orbit, drawn surely into the fire.

The rest of the retreat ran out like water down a drain, because Alison was not ready for contemplation, and had no idea what she would do with it if it happened to her. For a month she said her breath prayer, thinking only of what it felt like to have the cut mushrooms drop through her fingers, the green peppers shine when she washed them, the weeds in the garden fall like casualties of war when she separated them from the lettuce and carrots.

As she said her prayer and worked, the rest of her life fell away from the carrots and the peppers like a husk. She stopped thinking of Jack and his slow, sweet touch, of the promise that a translator would publish her poetry abroad, and of her husband's infidelity. Nothing was real but the pull of the carrot against the ground or the crumbling of the cheese if she cut it with less than total concentration. The breath prayer grew in her like sighs and tears, was expelled the same way, and Alison kept it in her mind all the time, close to her as the air. She saw the kittens' tails grow longer, the lettuce leaves stretch wider and said her words to herself, to God, to whoever was listening. "I'll stick with this prayer," she wrote in her journal. "I won't stop paying attention ever again."

At night she had more dreams, the dreams she had put aside during the day's pulling of weeds, the slicing of cheese. In one of them Jack became a dried-up old man, wrinkled and collapsed. He was not God anymore and Alison wondered how she had ever thought he was. The healing of her sore insides was under way; the plant was being watered. Alison was putting one foot in front of the other, not looking back.

3 WORDLESS PRAYER

"I am come into the world as light, so that everyone who believes in me should not remain in the darkness."

John 12:46

Like Alison, the other retreatants spent most of their time walking in a straight line. Heavy Brother Jonathan tried to fast, but faltered before the popovers cooked by Linda's sturdy daughter, and Anna worked grimly, like a prisoner promised freedom for good behavior, never smiling. After a few days, we got the hang of paying attention to the moment. Swaddled in the security of the Center, I became a little child sleeping long hours, walking with no destination in mind, forgetting there was anything to do next. Sometimes I would fall into step beside Michael, knowing no one would misunderstand my seeking out a man in his seventies, and we would silently roll the stones under our shoes as we walked, smiling at each other, glad for the company, saying hello and goodbye without words. Michael always seemed about to hug me at such times, as he did everyone else, but only shrugged, letting his hands fall at his sides and nodding his head.

At the Center, there was no next day or even next moment. Nothing to play, arrange or control. A bell rang when it was time to do the next task on the schedule. We were reduced to the now, which was all I securely had. If it rained, I sat by the window of my tiny, tar-papered room and stared out at the drops, falling with them, having nothing to do but fall. When the sun came out over the hills across the little road, I came out too, barefoot because my only pair of shoes had to be kept dry, and bathed my feet in the wet grass. If I could have looked forward to anything, I would have, but there was nothing, nothing. That is, there was nothing *else*. You had what was there, no more. It was useless to make up scenarios, counting tricks like a bridge player. You walked along the gravel road, feeling the stones under your feet, or wandered through the garden, looking at the dried bodies of last spring's roses, but nothing out of the way happened to immortalize the moment, freeze it like a wedding cake you could have back anytime. At home you could invite friends over, go to the theater, turn on the evening news. A touch away, something was in the wings, ready to happen to you.

The only life going on here was the inner life. For me, who had been alive only on the outside, the stillness, the absence of stimuli, was like being put in a coffin and laid underground. I understood what Jesus meant by dying like a grain of wheat, by being buried. What I had wanted was to be carried away in a rapture. What I got was to be dropped like a seed into ordinary ground, covered up and stamped on. All that I had been, all that I thought I was had been put to sleep, and whatever was left was strange and new to me, like all the things I was beginning to notice on my walks around the farm.

Along the side of the old clapboard house, spiders spun webs that hung dangerously from curls of peeling paint and shivered in the breezes from the lake. After a rain, I would go out and look at the webs through the magnifying glass Martin had given me, which I now wore around my neck to remind me not to miss anything, and to remind me that Martin thought nothing too small to be amazed at. I remembered following him through swamps and woods, swatting bugs and being stopped so I could inspect a handful of toadstools, held close to his face, while he looked at them through his magnifying glass. Martin saw nature the way I wanted to see God, as if there were nothing else but what he looked at. Because of him, I gave the spiders at the Center my full attention.

Unaware that they were working magic in a magic place, the spiders single-mindedly rebuilt their webs, their careless, busy legs popping raindrops at every move. They were like me, clumping through my own paradise in combat boots, with heavy weapons, celebrating nothing.

My breath prayer asked for help in loving the Lord, but it was also a way of asking help to love creation. Once I had believed holiness could happen only if you closed your eyes, sat on your hands and went from life to death in a plastic bag, hermetically sealed like a processed meal that is left uneaten in the freezer. My first Catholic friends, Hungarian émigrés, named Andrassy, had been admirers of saints who despised the body, like the one who sat 30 years on a pillar. The Andrassys had taught me how to "abandon the flesh," as they put it. They were a happy couple who summered on the Isle of Ischia, near Naples, and drank fine wine over their trout amandine. Lighting his imported Turkish cigarettes one after another, Gyuri would say to me, "Barbara, you must be pure as glass. Imitate Thérèse, the Little Flower, and burn out all the desires of the body. That is the way you must go." And he would light up again, as the conversation turned to the cost of living in Vienna, where he planned to retire. He left America to live in an apartment by the famous rose garden of Baden before he had explained to me how it was possible to walk through this world like a Desert Father or Oedipus, blind and penitent, while enjoying Turkish tobacco.

Watching the spider by the farmhouse reminded me of Teilhard de Chardin's belief that our work is to transform the world by making it conscious of itself in an act as natural as that of bees drawing honey from flowers and spiders spinning webs from their own juices. Scientists tell us that the material universe is running down the cosmic drain, its matter burning out. But they tell us too that nothing is lost or wasted. Matter doesn't vanish, but becomes energy, just as the food we eat becomes our blood, our bone, and the air becomes the electric power that drives our brains to make the world new, to give birth to God in the poor stable of our minds. The spider, with its eight feet stuck to the flat plane of its own cosmos, couldn't see the way the sun turned the drops on its web into a cartwheel of light. The fragile span under it was all it could know, while I was able to stand back and see a snowflake pattern of lights strung on invisible threads.

As I watched, I thought of the paths of all the retreatants as they wound through the world to the Center and now, as they walked from the kitchen to the garden to the chapel, weaving what I could perceive only in a series of nows, a confusion of random comings and goings. Linda and Peter, who knew what brought each of them to the farm and who set up the daily schedule, saw the whole web, but only God could see it as it was, a tissue of lives woven together and worn by the world.

Perhaps Peter could be gentle with us, because he knew where we were all coming from, though not where we were going—Father Paul, his heart still in the Brazilian jungle; Sister Anna, bleeding from childhood wounds; Therese, given so much love she was embarrassed at the generosity of God. Peter would have to find the right words for each of us, different as we were, and he found them. The words were always loving. In the past, spiritual directors often felt they had to be harsh in their zeal to get the heavy soul off the ground. They would prescribe penances, sacrifices, asceticism. "No bite, no cure," the old New England farmers used to say as they beat their children and drank bitter medicine. Peter seemed to understand that life lived without God, love or meaning was sadness enough. He didn't have to lay on us any more than was already there in order to make his point.

One afternoon we all sat around the picnic table waiting to hear how to make our half-hour of quiet prayer less chaotic, more centered. Many of us tended to confuse the tradition of orderly, disciplined mental prayer with self-expression. Our words put mind, imagination and emotion to work writing a novel which we read aloud to God. We called this self-indulgent exercise "talking to the Lord" and counted ourselves good or bad according to how much time we spent doing it. Peter explained that "talking to the Lord" had become almost the exclusive method of prayer in the West just when printed books and middle-class literacy rose in Europe. It was not that discursive mental prayer was bad, Peter told us, but that other forms of prayer were available, though eclipsed, in the Christian tradition, especially in the Eastern church, where wordless attention to the indwelling presence of God was the highest form of prayer, sought by desert monk and holy layman alike.

Peter paused in his talk and handed each of us a 12-inch square brown paper with a tiny gold circle in the center. We looked at it and then self-consciously at our neighbors, feeling as if we were in kindergarten again, playing with construction paper and shiny foil. Alison held the paper up against the sun from the window, trying to see if the thing were transparent. Melancholy Sister Anna put her fingertip over the gold dot and stared at the lightless square. Everyone seemed to understand that the simple homemade work of religious art would be his or her familiar companion throughout the next month, the only thing we had to call our own.

"An icon," Peter called the device, even though it had no face like the icons of Orthodox churches. No face, only light and empty space, centered in one small dot of gold. Undistracted by the beauty or symbolic value of the traditional icon, we were to empty our minds as we concentrated on the circle and be attentive to the presence of God within us. We were not to engage in self-study, consciousness-raising or regretting our sins, just to rest without distraction in God's hands.

"Concentration on the breath prayer will help you in point-gazing," Peter told us. "You've already started learning to concentrate, to put away useless thought. Now we want you to put away even the breath prayer. Just empty your minds as you watch the gold circle and wait. If thoughts come, accept them and let them go on their way. Instead of talking to God, let him talk to you."

Jane, the smartly dressed ex-nun, raised her hand. "This point-gazing sounds like quietism to me," she said. "Ignoring sin and temptation, resisting nothing. What happens if we start thinking sinful thoughts? Should we accept them, not fighting back? Not say all the prayers we know?"

"Don't be afraid that if you empty your mind, only ugly things will take over," Peter answered, writing something in his notebook. "Sure, you'll have temptations. Christ did too, during his 40 days of contemplation in the wilderness. The servant is no better than his master. But we have faith that if we knock, the door will be opened. Choose to empty your mind of all but God, put away daydreams, and have faith that God will fill you as he said he would. 'Blessed are the hungry,' the Lord told us, 'for they shall be filled.' Believe you will be too, for you wouldn't have come here if you weren't hungry, even though well-fed by the world's standards. Doing quite well, in fact."

Brother Jonathan blushed and looked down, sure Peter was talking to him, but then we all felt so. Not one of us could be called a failure, and a number of us were remarkably well off. Collectively, we could be called blessed, our measures packed down and flowing over, yet Peter was right. We had come because we were hungry for living bread. And despite the strangeness of their practices, Peter and Linda had been feeding the hungry for a long time, sending no one away empty. Like the Fathers in the desert who were sought after by disciples, and drawing on the same ancient traditions, the Sabbaths offered those who came not stones, but bread.

Knowing we would find point-gazing unfamiliar, Peter gave us a short history of the practice we were to try for the first time, referring not only to Christian tradition but the prayers of men and women in many times and places. The

Jews who prayed in the monastery at the foot of Mount Tabor focused their minds on a brass mirror or a round pool of water in order to still the thoughts which made a mess of their concentration. A Hindu might look at his elaborate mandala, while the Buddhist looks at a circle of clay. The idea is to get beneath the surface, to gaze not at the glass of a mirror, but at your reflection in it. For centuries, the Eastern church had venerated the icon, gold shining around the heads of saints, drawing the eye to the center, where the light was, and guiding the soul imperceptibly to the invisible source of that light. The Orthodox icon is a doorway to God; when you have entered by it, the door disappears as does everything that is not spirit. Disappearance of the material world, of course, was the whole purpose of the exercise, not to see visions or see anything at all, just to be emptied of all but God. Though the Sabbaths called their gold circle an icon, because its purpose was that of the ancient images of Linda's Ukrainian childhood, our devices were more like the Indian mandalas, on which the physical eyes gazed so long that the senses became overloaded, shut down, and the spiritual eyes took over, looking inward at the presence of God in the soul. It was this eyeless sight that we were trying to learn by gazing at Peter's little gold circles.

Peter wanted us to look at our gold circles for half-hour periods, focusing our minds on the bright dot in the brown square until thoughts of everything else receded like tide from shore. Always we began by reading scripture—only a verse or two, but enough to settle our minds on the task at hand. Distracting thoughts should be treated as St. Teresa of Avila said, "like a madman in the house." My thoughts were like those madmen of Teresa's, screaming, running around my brain in circles. Often I wondered if other people's minds were crazy rat's nests like mine, but was afraid to ask for fear I would be carted away. It was a new idea to me that random thoughts could be controlled by filling the ears with silence and the eyes with light.

Brother Jonathan looked uneasily around the room, and I guessed that he too had a mind full of madmen. He shifted his bulk, opened his mouth, then closed it, thinking better of his question. Therese was already sitting in front of her gold circle, leaning forward, hardly breathing, like a runner at the start of a race. It was hard to believe she had children at home, for she looked so like a child herself, ageless as an angel, though with shadows under her dark eyes that made them look very large. Therese had formed the habit of staying up to pray when everyone else was asleep, for it was the only time she had to herself in her busy household. Even on this retreat, which was for her a vacation, the shadows were still there.

As Peter taught us how to use the square with its bright center, I realized from the questions of the others that we were all unsure of what we would meet in that circle of light. For each one of us the time passed differently. Here is how it went for Therese, the young housewife.

4 THE STORY OF THERESE

For everyone that asks, receives, and he that
seeks, finds, and to him that knocks, it shall
be opened.

Luke 11:10

"Take five minutes," Peter said, looking at his watch
after each retreatant had settled in front of his or her gold circle. "Just clear your minds and let them rest."

Therese stared obediently, but at first her mind wouldn't
hold still. The chores she had left undone at home rose in her
head, occupying it like an army. She saw her two children,
six-year-old Tommy and three-year-old Karen, their faces
pale and sad, missing her. And Gary, her patient, tender husband, standing over them, holding her world together while
she stepped out of it for a time.

"A retreat at the Center is in order right now," Gary had
said one day, when Tommy's fit of temper was answered by
one of her own. "Call it a Mother's Day gift."

At the time, Therese had laughed and replied, "For
Christmas, I'll want an altar. And for my birthday? A chapel,
just for me." Gary was used to being asked for crazy things
by his beautiful, brooding wife and only smiled. She would
worry about saving money, remembering the frugal middle-
class home she had come from, then turn around and spend
every cent in her budget like a debutante. In marrying Gary,
Therese had married wealth and sometimes having so much
money made her nervous. Only last spring she had given the
Center a new tractor, glad she could help in their work, but
almost embarrassed at the lavishness of the gift. She wished it
could have been anonymous, like the money Gary had
donated through a priest to a girl whose teeth were falling
apart. But then her friends at the Center wouldn't know how

much she loved them. Always Therese had been unable to let the people close to her know. Sometimes she even had trouble telling God that he was loved and was glad he needed no words to read her heart.

As she looked into the tiny gold circle at the center of the brown square, Therese could see her own delicate face, with its high cheekbones, smooth, tanned skin and wide-spaced brown eyes. Her yellow hair was cut into short curls that framed her face, which people said looked like a Botticelli angel's. "Not an angel," she sighed, shaking her head a little, remembering how mad she got at Tommy, "not quite." Tommy was like her, too intense, too single-minded in his pursuit of what he wanted, while little Karen was gentle and sunny-tempered like her father. Perhaps her anger at Tommy, when he wanted to buy every toy in the store, was really at herself. She had always felt she would settle for nothing less than everything. Most people would have said she had it. But Therese knew better. Whatever God gave, she would never be satisfied until it was himself. Yet for God to give her that, she would have to give him all she had, all she was. Therese stirred restlessly, knowing she did not want to surrender that much.

Her eye was caught again by the center of the icon, which had picked up the light of the late afternoon sun. The circle was shining now, the brown background seemed to disappear. As she watched, forgetting now about the crush of images from her past, the gold center grew larger, filling her eyes until it seemed to pour into her. The bell rang, and Therese closed her eyes, not wanting to lose the light. When Peter asked each of them to speak in turn about what had happened during their five minutes of point-gazing, Therese prepared her answer, not wanting to tell what she had seen, but obedient as always.

Waiting for her turn, Therese felt the old fear of speaking out begin to wash over her. Fearing that his daughters might become forward if allowed to take part in adult conversations, her traditional father had for years been strict about what it was proper for a young lady to say aloud. Someone else, someone older and more experienced always knew best, and Therese had learned early to defer to authority. Perhaps because he had not heard her out during all their years together, Therese's father had been shocked and angry when she had gone to Montreal as a secretary. He had wanted her to become a nurse, but Therese was too sensitive to be only an arm's length away from suffering. As her father lay dying of cancer a few years later, and she suffered along with him, Therese knew how right she had been.

Her father had wanted her to go to college, having been deprived of it himself. Anxiously he watched his children for signs that they might be serious students, and he insisted that every one of them have a good education, however much it might cost him. He seldom spoke of God, but Therese was sure he believed God was to be feared more than loved. Though he went to confession every week, her father took Holy Communion only once a year, saying that no one was good enough to be intimate with God. He obeyed all the laws of the church, but showed no joy in doing so.

Her mother had left school after the eighth grade to help support her family and cared little about education. She had grown up on a farm in Quebec, as one of 12 children, daughter of an ex-seminarian and a beautiful, loving woman whom Therese remembered as always having a rosary near at hand. Therese's own mother, too, was devoted to Mary and shared her love with her daughters. Both Therese's parents cared for and protected her like benevolent, reliable gods, as Gary was to do later. Over her 28 years, Therese had come to feel that others were responsible for making her happy. She knew this was a fault and worried about it. Like other childish notions, it would have to be given up. St. Paul's words were hers: "When I was a child, I spoke as a child, but now that I am a man, I have put away childish things." She would have to put away the idea that other people were in charge of her happiness.

In spite of all their trying, they had not succeeded, Therese sighed. God was different: He made demands, wanted her to grow up, take charge of herself and of her life so she could hand it over to him. "You can't give up what you don't have in the first place," she told herself and then realized Robert was nudging her to speak. Stammering a little, she said something about the gold circle getting bigger as she watched but couldn't talk of how the light had streamed into her.

The break was over, and the group sat again before the icons, this time for 15 minutes. Now Therese was becoming more confident and less afraid of surrendering. As she entered the chapel, she had placed herself firmly in the hands of Jesus, and now she felt safe. Expecting to see again the light growing in the center of the square, she concentrated with all her strength on her gold circle. This time she saw shadows shift over the surface of it and disappear, leaving a man's bearded profile. The center was glowing again, and as she watched, trying to keep her breathing smooth and deep as Peter had instructed her, she saw the face become a laughing woman's. She leaned forward, wondering who she was seeing. Was the bearded man Jesus? Was the woman herself? Her mind began to boil with questions, and she had to make an effort to keep the lid on. Suddenly, the face appeared as half-male, half-female, split down the middle into two profiles, the back of one head melting into the back of the other, becoming a single person. The edges of the brown square turned dark brown as though they were burnt. She did not understand what she was seeing, but felt safe. Leaning back against the wall, she fell asleep and woke up just in time for the 5:30 service.

It was Thursday, the day Peter and Linda led a Healing

of Memories session after Mass, during which the retreatants reviewed their past lives and forgave those who had hurt them. Therese dreaded it, knowing which memories were going to be brought up. She moved her chair into the semicircle made by the others and felt a firm hand on her shoulder. Without looking around, she felt sure it was Linda's and was glad. Linda was strong, like a mother, and Therese wanted somebody strong to pray for her.

She remembered how she had left her secretarial job, with no savings in her pocket, and volunteered for the frontier apostolate in Manitoba. Her father was furious, and let her know it. Not only had she gone against his wish to see her an educated professional, but she was wandering through life like a demented hippie. Therese had never stood up to him before, but knew she had to make it clear she listened to God first, not her father. When her mother died a year later of a sudden heart attack, Therese felt her father's pain and loneliness as her own. She herself had left him, and now he had no one. Conscious again of the hand on her shoulder, Therese took a deep breath and brought back the memory of the dark time after her mother's death, when God had ceased to speak to her. The Eucharist was only a hard, dry thing stuck in her throat like the grief she couldn't share with anyone, not even Gary.

The man who was to be her husband had volunteered his services as a teacher to the apostolate at the same time as Therese, who had offered herself with no particular idea of what she would do. She wound up working first in the school kitchen and then as the parish secretary. The apostolate was not the peaceful place she had hoped to find. The priests argued with one another, the community argued with the priests. These people could not teach her how to open her heart and communicate love. When the strain and hard work broke her health, she went home to Quebec. Again, her father urged her to stay, but she believed God wanted her back in the apostolate. Leaving her father, she wept, for she felt there was little time left for them to open their hearts to each other.

As the face of her father came to mind, his eyes looking deep into hers, Therese blocked the memory rising in her. She did not want to remember how he had died. Linda's voice went on softly from somewhere behind her. "Lord, take away the guilt and anger of our young adulthood, our quarrels with our families and the pain they caused us." Therese wanted to hold her aching head in her hands. It hurt as though all the bad memories were banging at it like a door. Only her will kept the door closed. She would not remember that death which had almost been followed by her own, and would have been, if not for Gary.

After dinner, Therese stayed outside for a long time, playing with Philo the collie, who lay on his back and put his feet foolishly in the air, nudging her arm with his long nose as she tickled him. The grass felt cool and soft under her bare legs, and when Philo had been tickled to sleep, she curled up beside him next to the broken-down gray fence and slept too. In her dreams, Gary was leaving her for other women. Why was he angry at her? she wondered, as she woke up shaking in the evening chill, wrapping her arms around herself. Gary was never angry. But maybe he had a right to be. Other women settled down and were glad with less than she had, but Therese was restless, never satisfied. How did Gary feel, knowing he alone could not make her happy? She must have hurt him, she thought, and she would go on hurting him until she knew how to stop hurting herself.

Reluctantly, she went into the chapel for the evening session and looked at her gold circle, seeing again the familiar, bearded face. Therese leaned forward, watching the single face break into many. "I am the vine and you are the branches." The words of Jesus sprang into her mind and the bearded man was back again, this time holding a baby. Who was the baby? Was it herself, a grown woman with two babies of her own? She shook her head, still seeing her children holding out their hands, needing her, needing what she herself needed. She had wanted to be for them a doorway to God, but doorways were empty, open, and she was not. To be that, she would have to put away childish things, but some part of her stubbornly hung onto her lost childhood, her lost father.

Therese remembered how it had felt to learn she no longer had a father. It was time she let the memory of his death come to the surface and be healed like the others. Her father had died of cancer, in 1975, only a year after his wife. It had been a terrible death, stretched out over four months. Therese's tears ran down her face. She had sat by his side, feeling his pain, as unable to speak to him as he was to her. Here was this stern, gaunt man from whom she had grown like a seed, part of him, not her own at all, and neither of them could express whatever love they felt. Throughout his drugged sleep, Therese wept silently with her face in her hands, losing him moment by moment, and knowing her loss.

After the funeral, Therese took an overdose of pills and alcohol not wanting to kill herself but only to sleep for a long time. Gary understood what sort of sleep it was and sped to the hospital with her, waiting at her side till her stomach was pumped, until even her soul seemed emptied out. Then he took her home to their farm, holding her tight the whole way, loving the sad, lost thing she had become, loving what she would be.

Gary had always known what she needed. When she had despaired at the apostolate, working under a drunk, lazy cook, Gary had stood by, waiting to help her as he had helped so many others. When they had first gone out together, she had no idea that he was falling in love with her. Gary was the same way with everybody as with her. Many girls were drawn to him, and he was always gentle with their feelings. When he asked Therese to marry him, she said yes, trusting that he would be gentle with her too. She had not been disappointed, though she had begun the marriage thinking she should be hearing harpstrings and smelling flowers all the time. She expected Gary to perform daily miracles to keep her happy. Now, sitting on her cushion at the Center, face to the wall, she saw him more clearly than if he were present in the flesh—a patient, simple man, waiting with his hands out. No harpstrings, no flowers.

Therese's head hurt again as she seemed to see Gary's figure on the icon, his hands open to her, full of good things. As she looked, the bearded man became visible behind Gary, shining through him, beckoning to her. She began to cry again, the tears heavy as fingers on her face. Her body became like a statue, weighed down with self and with the will that had propelled her through life like a motor for almost 30 years. She hardly breathed, feeling the motor run down and stop. The bearded man was still there, looking into her face, and she was ashamed of having offered him so little. Here she was with her soul hanging in rags, like a beggar late in the day with no coins in his cup. She was empty, empty.

Therese felt a sudden rush of energy rise like fire to the center of her body and wrap her heart in warmth. She closed her eyes and there seemed to be light caught under her lids. Without seeing him, she felt close to Tommy, her strong-willed little son. If only she could love him as God loved him, be present to him like air, knowing that God was his Father and food, being an open door between them. "Let Tommy go." The words came to her cool and spattering like rain. "Let Tommy alone," she heard in the wordfall. Therese answered, remembering her words later, though at the time there seemed to be no words at all. "He's yours, not mine," she said. "He came to me naked and small." She caught her breath. "That's how I came to you, Lord, the same way. We are so small we curl up in the palm of your hand, God. And when we are full of you, we are so big the world can't hold us." To be big, to be strong and full-grown no longer seemed to Therese a fearful thing. She opened her hands slowly and raised them, palms up, feeling the children take one side of her, Gary the other, not as if they were pulling her apart, but putting her back together. Nothing of her was left in between, and she folded her hands together like an empty cup, glad, not missing what had fallen out. She watched the face in the icon's golden circle drop into a well of light and become living water, to be drunk by anyone who was thirsty.

5 PRAYER OF LISTENING

"For behold, the kingdom of God is within
you."

Luke 17:21

Therese's experience with point-gazing was not unusual,
as I learned later from other journals. None of us expected
anything, because we had been taught all our lives that only
great ascetics could hope for ecstatic experiences. And they
would apparently have to whip themselves or eat locusts for
20 years before encountering God directly. We were more
like Moses, surprised by the burning bush. Except by the
deep, unstoppable desire of our hearts which had driven us to
the Center in the first place, we were not prepared for
miracles. Spiritual graces were only words in books for most
of us, and we sat staring self-consciously at our brown
squares, embarrassed at the simplicity of the method, the
childishness of our obedience. Though we had almost all
been thoroughly in charge of running our own lives, we were
quick to obey, however silly the exercise might seem, the
more so because Peter was so reluctant to demand anything
of us.

In my case the sudden lifting of responsibility had left me
groggy and slow to move, as if my mind had gone to sleep
and no other faculty were well enough developed to take its
place. Only at night, in dreams, did the old hectic, anxious
self return. At the Center, it seemed I was awake while sleeping, and asleep while awake. Because my mind slept during
the day, the rest of me had to learn how to be awake. I
relearned how to walk by paying attention to where I put my
feet, relearned eating by paying attention to the texture of the
food, all the while breathing slowly and deeply, saying my
breath prayer. When my mind wandered to dancing with

Martin or to my fall teaching syllabus, I would pull it back gently like a straying child. The world seemed as strange to me as if I were an infant or some creature from outer space. For the first time Jesus' words became clear to me: "Unless you become as little children, you shall not enter the kingdom of heaven." I was coming to understand that the "kingdom of God is within you," and that you have only to be still to be there, getting your mind off your chattering, demanding, rattled self. Gazing on the golden circle offered us the way inside ourselves and out again, as if we were going in through the little hole in the middle and bodilessly out on the other side into unlimited light.

We tried not to be aware of our surroundings, or of our companions, and gazed at our circles with slightly unfocused eyes as we had been told to do, as if we were looking behind, not at the surface of the brown paper.

I tried not to notice Michael on one side of me, deep-breathing like an athlete, the air whistling in his wrinkled throat, and Brother Jonathan on the other side, his mouth slightly open, the sweat running down his plump cheeks into it. Only the three of us sat on chairs, while most of the others sat on plump flowered cushions, like monks in a Buddhist *zendo*. All of us faced the walls of the half-finished chapel, having placed our icons at eye level between the beams, against the bare wood planks.

The first three-minute trial offered nothing but the sensation of a spreading circle, which I took to be an optical illusion. Peter asked us to report what we had seen, and went around the room, hearing from each one. Like most of the retreatants, I had nothing to report, and felt envious of the few who had seen glowing cartwheels or tunnels of bright light. Convinced I would never see anything but a small gold circle in a large brown square, I sighed and returned to my "prayer of listening," this time for a five-minute period. Suddenly my eyes opened wide and I sat straight up, staring. Either my square had gone crazy or I had.

My journal entry, written a half-hour later, contains a fresh account of the event.

July 9, 5:15 p.m.
(five-minute session)

No initial effect and no expectation of one. Though I kept my eyes focused on the central circle, I was aware that the edges of the square were darkening like burning leaves. From behind the square, light streamed out, as sun does behind a cloud. The sight was so striking, I checked to see if sunbeams were coming through the window behind me, illuminating the square, but the window was darkened by the shadow of the mountain. I turned back. The light was still there, and the golden center of the square was beginning to bulge like a supernova, when the bell rang signalling the end of the five minutes. A feeling of intense interest, surprise and well-being came over me. I was aware of doing nothing to originate or sustain either the phenomenon or its exhilarating effects.

(After ten-minute session)

The outside of the square again began to shine, but this time with darting red and gold bars, rimming the edges with rainbow colors in a small halo around it. For a second I glanced at Brother Jonathan's square, checking to see if it had gone crazy too. His looked quite ordinary to me, as did mine, when I gazed at it again.

The power of this exercise should have been obvious to me, as well as the dangers of practicing it without a director. But six months afterward, when Linda heard I had taught it to a number of people she emphasized the importance of a good spiritual director, warning me of cases where point-gazers fell apart or were invaded by subtle, malevolent influences. The Orthodox fathers warned that using such repetitive practices without spiritual guidance might actually lead to insanity, especially if the practitioner were not leading a holy, disciplined life, which supported the pure intention of the practice. When a person drops below the conscious mind into areas of his own being where no protections, no controls, exist, he can drown in the surge of repressed images, sexuality and night terrors. Even worse, he may experience being possessed by demonic forces or transported out of the body, unable to get back in. To me these melancholy warnings sounded like the stuff of horror films. But Linda believed in their reality and urged us to take no chances. The soul at prayer, she said, is not a mere vacuum, but actively loving, full of faith and obedient to divine law. Jane needn't have worried about quietism. Linda's point-gazing was to be the stillness of an athlete running in place to remain strong while he waited to begin to race.

Along with having a director you can trust who can discern any demons or dementia, Linda said, the point-gazer ought to make it a practice to begin his or her prayer of quiet with a verse from scripture with which to fix the intention on the task at hand, giving it unreservedly to Christ. Each time we sat down in the chapel for our half-hour prayer of listening, one of our group walked up to the Bible on the lectern and read the assigned verse, always with some reference to light, such as the words from the gospel of John: "The Word was the source of life, and this life brought light to mankind."

Light was the Center's symbol of God's presence. Little was said about the dark night of the soul, though toward the end of the retreat we heard tapes by a woman hermit in Maine quoting St. John of the Cross: The way to meet God is through darkness and unknowing. For the most part, we were given the teachings of the Eastern Orthodox saints, like St. Simeon the New Theologian, who wrote in a hymn:

> I continually see the light by night and by day. Day appears like night to me, and night is day. I do not want to sleep.

In this light one sees God and is seen by him. The emphasis at the Center was not on darkness, not on the time of crucifixion, but on the light of Easter Morning. Perhaps because

Eastern spirituality was not so interlaced with rationalism as that of the West, going through the darkness was not a necessary step. In any case, the spiritual sources at the Center were almost entirely joyful. We lived simply, but not as ascetics. Food was available whenever we wanted it, and extra sleep was encouraged, especially for those of us who had been under heavy stress during the past working year. We even had a party halfway through the retreat.

It was Sunday, and a Mass was said outside, after which we had a picnic dinner and were first allowed to talk to one another. By now we were eager to find out whatever we could in this brief time about what lay behind each silent, familiar presence. We didn't ask all we wanted to and smiled a lot, realizing after each short conversation that we had known one another better in silence than we could now with words. As if to show us how unnecessary words were, animals crashed our party and took over. Toby, the young ram who was usually penned behind the farmhouse, came trotting down the long front porch, his pointed hoofs clattering on the wood, terrifying Sister Anna, who ran inside. Usually Toby tried to shove his way through the screen door into the dining room, his bland, half-amused face thrust forward like a football player's on the offensive. Whoever had educated me about the peaceful nature of sheep had been wrong. Toby was a fierce sheep, one who would never be led to the slaughter without a fight. He had one broken horn, and he tipped the other at a rakish angle as he lunged at us. Toby was formidable, and I felt like hiding behind a tree when he joined the party.

Toby visited us during the T'ai Chi exercise in which another retreatant and I demonstrated the ancient Chinese "moving meditation," and explained its power to center the body as well as to settle the mind. Afterward we all stood in a circle on the lawn, practicing the simple T'ai Chi moves, solemn and slow as a ballet of glaciers. Into our circle Toby charged, ears laid back, pointed hoofs flying, chased by

Philo, who had suddenly remembered his ancestral programming to assert his authority over any unorthodox sheep in the neighborhood. He and Toby fenced and parried in the middle of our circle, with Toby refusing to be moved, shoving his horn at a painful angle into Philo's thick chest fur. We watched anxiously, afraid the big, gentle dog would be hurt by this desperate sheep.

Even the sheep around here break the rules, I thought, seeing Toby dance dangerously on his sharp hoofs and glare at Philo. In fact, there were no rules. We were on our own to be whatever we were, like Toby. Linda and Peter had no preconceived notion of the sort of saints we might become. They themselves had broken a lot of rules in their time, though they were now obedient to a rule of selflessness as absolute as any monk's. With a last triumphant lunge, Toby threw himself against Philo, who rolled over on his back and stuck his four feet cravenly in the air. We all applauded, glad for the overturning of rules, and for the dignity of all sheep when under pressure. With the humiliation of poor Philo, the three-hour reprieve was over, and we returned to silence and to avoiding one another's eyes.

Since I washed lunch dishes with Brother Jonathan, eye contact was inevitable. He would wag his head knowingly when an encrusted pan was presented to be washed and whisper to me the preposterous reprisals he planned against the cooks. He was a Toby, a sheep who wouldn't be herded, and would end by turning all authority upside down if he had his way. When I first sat across from Brother Jonathan at dinner, I was repelled by the food he heaped on his plate, by his going back for seconds or for bread. "Might as well slap it right on your tum, Piggy," I thought furiously, wanting him to see how bad he was. Fat people had always disgusted me. I thought them weak-willed, convicted publicly of their sin, while the rest of us enjoyed our more concealable vices. Later I began to love Piggy and watched his efforts at self-control as anxiously as a coach watching his pet tailback going for a goal. "Don't do it Piggy," I'd say under my breath as he pushed back his chair, lusting for one more chunk of corn-bread. When he would return to the table, his plate full of let-tuce, I would be relieved and glad. "Good for you, Piggy," I'd think. "Right on." Or if he would fall from grace and heap his plate with spaghetti, miserably sticking his face close to it until the plate was empty, I would feel a heavy sorrow and mutter into my virtuously sugarless tea, "God, help him not to want it so much. Help him not to want anything so much as he wants that spaghetti."

Each one of us felt the urge to hold up the other, the way elephants lean against a wounded comrade between them, supporting him to safety. Brother Jonathan's food-lust was no worse than my people-lust, my urge to possess securely each person I cared about. His was the more innocent of the two obsessions. As I watched him, the fat people in my history suddenly seemed to me not ugly but like beaming suns, rising with fullness and life, not to be despised ever again. And so we became a good family, holding each other's hands, cheering at each other's small victories.

The extended family growing at the Center was for me a living image of Christ's body, the vine of which we were the branches. In the one-eyed squint of Western rational culture we are separate beings. In the binocular vision of less com-plicated cultures, each apparently separate soul is seen in three-dimensional depth against a background of other souls, bodies, trees, flowers, stones. Our ordinary five senses perceive the obvious separateness, the skin that wraps up each complicated bundle of flesh and bone. A glimpse into the electron-microscope, however, shows us a whirling mass of particles containing vast empty spaces and connected by energy patterns that leap these distances as light leaps in-tergalactic space. Kirlian photography reveals a field of energy hovering around us that takes on the intensity and quality of our feelings, mingling with the auras spreading from other human and animal forms until we do not know where we leave off and our neighbor begins. So when Brother Jonathan ate too much spaghetti, I felt too full. When he sat beside me in the chapel, I matched my breathing to his. What Brother Jonathan reminded me of was the claim of the body, its weight and insistent need. Looking at him, I felt the heft of a lifetime's desires, appetites and the urge to consume the world rather than to appreciate it, to let it be.

6 THE STORY OF JONATHAN

Nothing the world has to offer
—the sensual body,
the lustful eye,
pride in possessions—
could ever come from the Father
but only from the world;
and the world, with all it craves for,
is coming to an end;
but anyone who does the will of God
remains for ever.

1 John 2:16-17

One day Jonathan took a walk and crashed through the fragile bridge on the way to the fields and woods back of the Center. The other men had to spend a day repairing the damage, and Jonathan blushed at the smiles that followed Peter's announcement of the task. Everybody knew which one of us had been responsible. His was a cautionary tale of the flesh overcoming fleshly gravity as a stumbling block to sanctity. Yet, he contained within himself more of creation than any of us. He seemed to have an urge to take as much as possible into his body, accepting all of it, making it a part of him, denying access to nothing.

Brother Jonathan was not at fault for trying to eat up the whole world; he had merely gone about it in the wrong way. In the end, he learned to eat it with no more than his eyes and his heart, without any lust for possession. Like Elijah he had been filled beyond need with bread in the wilderness. Instead of being an emblem of our failure to see body and mind as one thing, Jonathan's body became for him a sign of his spirit's fullness, its overflow into the physical world, abundant and pure, like a stream struck by Moses from a rock.

Jonathan had always known what his real sins were, even as a child, when he asked precocious questions and made clever jokes about the answers. The answers given always rankled in him. "What is the Immaculate Conception?" he would ask his mother, a convert from Methodism. "If a body is perfect and has a perfect soul in it, why wouldn't her body just fade away, go sort of transparent?" He thought of all the gauzy pictures of Mary on the walls at school. "What's the use of the body once you're perfect? It just makes trouble."

His mother was from an old New England family, and like its members had lived a life of heroic discipline and order. She slapped Jonathan's hand smartly as it crept over to the pie crust she was rolling out on the counter. "The body is like a school," she said, flattening the dough to uniform thinness. "It's suffering that teaches us to turn away from the world of flesh so that we can love God alone. In heaven we'll get a perfect body, like Jesus and Mary, but until then, we have to use discipline. No, don't eat raw pie crust. It will sit in your stomach and make you sick."

Jonathan propped his round pink face on his hands and leaned his elbows on the counter, staring sorrowfully at the white crescents his mother was lopping off the edge of the crust. The message was clear. What you craved for the body's pleasure couldn't become part of your soul's growth. The only bridge between body and soul was suffering. Pleasure was beside the point and might even be a way the devil could get at you.

His father was a second-generation Irish-American who was firmly grounded in the traditional view of the soul's war against the flesh. His duty was to keep the soul in charge, beating down the rebellions of the stubborn body, as he disciplined the rising willfulness of his four spirited children for their own good.

Jonathan learned early that disobedience was frowned

upon, but because he was a clever boy, he also learned how to avoid trouble. He had a quick wit and tongue and could make people approve of him by making them laugh. He became a good boy, following orders outwardly, but inside himself, he went his own way. At least they couldn't punish you for eating too much, and Jonathan began early to stuff himself at the table and between meals. As he grew older, he was mocked at school for being fat, but was able to disarm his tormentors with clowning. Because he was bright and dutiful in his studies, the sisters and brothers who were his teachers encouraged him in his desire to become a priest. But he dropped out of minor seminary after one and a half years because of chronic, worsening asthma. As he fought for air, hanging over a pailful of steaming water, breathing the vapor that opened his clogged bronchioles, Jonathan would imagine himself free of the crushing weight of substance, free of constraints, light and rising vaporously from the prison of matter. "Wretched man that I am," he groaned with St. Paul, "who will deliver me from this body of death?"

His ailing body kicked against the pricks, furious at the efforts being made on all sides to reduce him to obedience and sameness with the others. In retaliation he ate even more, spreading out into the world instead of shrinking as the church told him to do. He would not openly rebel against either God or family, but quietly and with systematic thoroughness ate his way through Catholic high school and college as he had through the religious grammar schools of his early childhood. He watched the other boys fall into sins which got them suspended or even prematurely married and knew he had chosen the safest course.

Not until he was in his mid-twenties did he enter a delayed adolescence. By then he had become a Christian Brother and a teacher of teen-agers. Among them he was in his element. They laughed at his clowning, shared his distrust of authority and loved to play as much as he did. He lived through a second boyhood with them, this time leading from strength, no longer shy or fearful as he had been in his own school days.

With his fellow teachers, too, he put down roots, developing deep friendships. His community was rich soil, nourishing its members with love, and Jonathan was happy soaking up that love. When some of his friends, shaken by the changes in the church, began to leave the order, Jonathan felt a hollow in himself like that left by a pulled tooth. He would sit after supper, staring out of the window looking at the empty road along the brothers' residence, wondering what would happen if he packed his bag and walked down that road to a life alone, unshaped by anyone but himself. Why had he become a religious, anyway? Perhaps only because going out into the world was too much for him. Among the brothers, he was protected, as if by a big, devoted family. Sex was forbidden, it was true, but all other pleasures were allowed. He could eat, play games, tell jokes, listen to music and read. For Jonathan, with his modest expectations from this world, the terms were acceptable. Yet he felt in his heart a vague longing for love, for a passion that would draw him out of himself and make him a transcendent being, dignified, beautiful and no longer a poor, fat, restless brother. He had hoped that his lover would be God, but God had made himself scarce. If he left the order, perhaps he could find a good woman with whom to make a life. Then, looking down at himself, he shook his head, doubting that any girl would have him. And if one did, would she be enough to fill him up? Marriage might be like trying to get enough to eat which he never seemed able to do. Always he wanted more than there was. No, God it would have to be. God or nobody. He would follow his first love and not turn back like the friends who had left the order one by one.

Instead of continuing to teach academic subjects as he had done since graduating from college, Jonathan resolved to teach religion and took his M. A. in religious education at a university in New England. There he was thrown with other restless, searching men and women and drawn into the movement protesting the Vietnam war. At last his dissatisfaction with authority, which had kept him hobbled and powerless all his life, had found a focus. In a brave gesture, Jonathan returned his draft card to the Selective Service office and waited with a sort of exalted terror to be made an example of. But since he was a religious, no one dragged him off to jail or even fined him. Like his church in an increasingly secular society, he was simply ignored. Again the walls of authority and tradition began to close in on him as they had always done. Where in this world was the adventure, the freedom, the natural, unfettered gaiety he saw in the children of the sixties, who left all institutions and customs behind for a New Jerusalem created by their instincts and their drugs? By the early seventies, Jonathan had become depressed and frustrated, still staring at the road outside his window, still empty and longing to be filled.

The charismatic movement, offering its rush of love and happy release in tears, gave him new hope, for in this ecstasy, this self-surrender with a group of laughing, crying friends, raising their hands to God, embracing each other as they felt the Spirit sweep through them like an electrical storm, he seemed for a while to find the way out of his own mind trap. For some time and with growing discomfort he had realized that his prison had not been built by the authorities of church, family or government, but by his own rigorous, conventionally analytical mind, which wanted to control and organize the shifting currents of ordinary life. It was like trying to harness the tides of the ocean to run a sawmill. Jonathan's body, with its own wisdom, rebelled against the feverish plans of the separated intellect in charge of operations. He became ill, his blood pressure shooting up dangerously.

He answered a call to work in the inner city, loving the young people who were crazy, free, their own masters. His spiritual life, however, began to flounder. He felt choked by the rule-ridden community in which he lived. Again his blood pressure began to climb as his body knocked on the door of his soul, waiting to be heard. Some of his new friends spoke of a spiritual renaissance going on at the Thomas Merton Center in Canada, and Jonathan was determined to be part of it. Serving the poor was good, teaching the ignorant about God was good, but unless he learned to give himself and his will entirely to God, he would go on kicking against the goad. While to others he seemed a modest, humble man, Jonathan knew the truth: He was proud—proud of his brains, his vocation, his life of service. He was full of himself, fat and heavy with self, yet wanting to be full of God. And so he came to the Center, where he heard himself murmuring like John the Baptist, "He must increase, I must decrease."

The breath prayer he chose was as earthy and literal as he could make it: "Father, mold me as your son." He wanted to be stripped down to nothing, pared, transformed; and he wanted that transformation both in body and soul, knowing at last that the two were one thing. As he worked in the kitchen washing dishes or prepared greeting cards at the picnic table, he said his prayer, feeling each step as one toward home, with a long way to go but no urge to run. He said his prayer as he walked in the warm rain which seemed like heaven communicating with earth, soul with body.

When he sat before his gold circle the first time, he seemed to see light at the end of a tunnel, with the word "you" in big letters on the dot that disappeared into some infinite hole in the space behind the paper. As the days went on, point-gazing became a descent into some deep, unknown part of himself, one full of light and calm. Like a child leafing through a picture book, he saw the forms of animals in the light of the circle. They were figures in a fiery furnace—first fish, then frogs, then fish again. He felt as though he were sinking into a preconscious, primeval past, before his ego had set out to eat up the world, before he had left the womb of his mother. Though his body felt hot and itchy on the hard chair, Jonathan found that the time in chapel moved swiftly. He breathed slowly and deeply, his eyes fixed on the circle, surer and surer that he was in the presence of God. As time went on, images faded, and the brown square with its dot of gold was merely a reminder of God's presence, nothing in itself.

In Jonathan's dreams, all his sins began to come to the surface in scenarios too wild to be devised by his waking imagination, and he woke up with a start, bumping his head against the post of the narrow bunk bed. He dreamed the pope visited the Christian Brothers school. As Jonathan came downstairs to greet the pontiff, a strange girl seized his sleeve and begged him for something to eat. "Go find a good restaurant," he told her and pulled his sleeve away. Never before had it occurred to him that while he was eating more than any three men needed, others were starving. The pope looked at him with sad, reproachful eyes, and Jonathan sat up in bed, staring at the unblinking moon that shone through the window.

The next day in the chapel, Jonathan did not try as hard as usual to be alert, but simply made himself present. Suddenly he felt his shoulders become heavy, as if his body was fighting the gravity of Jupiter, and his chest sank as if it would crush his heart. He breathed slowly and deeply. No images crossed the brown square now, and Jonathan saw a quick ray of light pass between the circle and his own heart, piercing him like a needle.

Jonathan destroyed the bridge on the next day, and to him it seemed a good sign. He was breaking with an old self, changing what he was to what he would be. Only half embarrassed, he helped the other men make a new bridge and smiled as he lifted the beams. He felt alive and well, as though like a diligent ant he were building the earth, one speck of dust at a time and himself with it, inseparable from it. That evening in the chapel he felt a rush of heat from his lower body to his heart, which swelled to bursting. For a moment he feared that his high blood pressure had erupted again and would finish him off. Then the presence of the Lord came over him, and he felt with gladness that Christ was as happy to be with him as he was to be with Christ. He wanted to be totally absorbed into the heart of Jesus, dissolved like a drop of water in wine, and he was.

An image came to him of himself as a child of six, watching his father build a boat in which Jonathan was to journey someday across a large body of water. His father promised to come along, but said Jonathan might not be able to see him. All Jonathan would have to do was to steer, his father said, but the boat's sail had a will of its own, if Jonathan could only wait patiently to know what that was. Sitting on the hard chair, caught up in the light that seemed to stream from the gold circle, Jonathan felt he was on the journey even now, crossing over the depths of his own mind to reach some other, happier shore than the one on which he had lived his whole life. In the vision, he trusted his father and the boat, and the 40-year-old Jonathan found himself trusting too, ready for anything, even total solitude.

He was prepared for the hermitage, a small cabin out in the woods, where for 24 hours, a retreatant went to be empty and alone. Jonathan, who loved the company of others, even when not allowed to talk to them, had often passed by the shabby little building, averting his eyes, not wanting to imagine himself trapped inside. Now he thought of the single, bare room as a mansion, one of those God had prepared for those who love him, one that would be home.

Before he went to the hermitage for his day and night of solitude, Jonathan had a bad dream in which he saw a face like his own, but disfigured, rush past him out of the room, ugly as a devil. He awoke in fear, making the sign of the cross, wondering if this hateful twin were only a dream. Perhaps the evil image would come back when he was alone in the hermitage. Perhaps it was a self too deeply rooted in him to be displaced even by God. Jonathan was uneasy and made the sign of the cross again before getting up to prepare for his time in the desert. Deliberately he took only bread and water and ate no breakfast before he left. From Peter and Linda he had learned to consecrate his food, not simply devour it, and to put himself in God's presence gently as he would place a baby bird back in its nest. The hermitage, he felt, would be his nest.

About that time alone, his journal says nothing but the words of St. Paul: "I live, no longer I, but Christ in me." He came back to the farmhouse resolving to be totally present to the Lord all his life. Jonathan had found the Lover he was looking for.

In his journal Jonathan wrote these words about his last day at the Center:

> The day was filled with the realization that I've reached the end of the beginning. Calm, joyous, yet bittersweet. Must we come down from the mountain? Yes. Yet it was only a foothill to Mt. Carmel. So I must go from here—hopeful, confident that my Guide goes with me and that he will lead me by the right path to where he has no place to lay his head. "To whom shall we go, O Lord? Your words are the words of eternal life." Help me to listen!—Amen.

7 WAR, IN SILENCE

Who is my neighbor? . . .
"The one who took pity."
Luke 10:29,37

Alone in the hermitage, Jonathan had learned that he was part of a family. Not until then did he understand what he was receiving from the rest of us, and what he was giving in return. When I say that the Center was a family, it's not meant in an altogether positive way. Linda was the mother of us all, and we competed for her attention. She was hidden most of the time in her "secret annex," as I mentally christened the rustic, sunlit apartment behind the old plank door near the kitchen, with its "private" sign. It was hard to catch her eye, but we tried. One visiting priest, who had been on the month-long retreat two years before, confessed to us during an informal chapel talk that his retreat had been highly competitive.

"We all wanted to be first to see a vision," he said, stretching out his long legs and fiddling with the horns of his heavy dark-rimmed glasses. "Whoever saw the most light and could report his visions most convincingly got noticed. You couldn't help wanting to get feedback."

Linda, who wasn't in hiding at the moment, shrugged, spreading her hands, in what I imagined was a middle-European gesture learned from her Ukrainian father. "It's true that people compete even for spiritual booty," she said. "But we don't encourage it. This ego of ours, this false self, is like a brat, making a fuss because it's insecure. All bravado and showing off. No place to rest its head. Root the self in God and the ego goes to sleep like a good, tired child. I've told you before, and you'll hear it again, that the lights and visions don't mean a thing, and they don't stay. Some of the strongest retreatants, whose lives change the most, see nothing at all. They don't see light. Other people see the love of God shining out of them. That's all that matters in the long run—how transparent you are to the love of God, how empty of everything else. Then you don't care if you're noticed or not. A light doesn't see itself burn."

We had come to this silent paradise, Linda was telling us, to experience being loved without earning anything, without being anyone special, but sometimes we forgot why we had come. Jane, the academic ex-nun, and I forgot fairly often, perhaps because we both wanted to shine. Even in Eden there are snakes, and our competition was one of them. Jane had been to the Center before, and knew the ropes. She had a strong will, a bright mind, and a driving ambition to be the best. Like me, she was a teacher, and was used to having the last word in arguments. During our rare roundtable discussions about the tradition of contemplative life in the church, Jane and I traded theories and information the way boxers trade blows. Scholarship was only one area of competition. We were both good singers and at Mass would try to out-sing each other, belting out the responses. She had a stronger, deeper voice, but I could go higher. Who won the day's competition depended on the vocal range of the songs chosen by Peter in holy ignorance of the duel going on between his two competitive retreatants. Other areas of warfare were staked out during the occasional question-and-answer sessions.

On the third day of the retreat, we sat around the picnic table discussing our reaction to the work schedule. Jane and I were at opposite ends, as usual. Robert, whom I had seen baretopped and beautifully gleaming with sweat on the roof the day before, leaned his bearded chin in his hand and confessed with a bit of shame that he was afraid he had been compulsive again.

"I find myself working too hard," he said, when Peter asked us to talk about our use of the breath prayer during our two hours of morning work. "It's always this way. I want someone to pat me on the head and love me for knocking myself out. So I scraped off paint until the last minute, hating it, getting tired and angry. The breath prayer wasn't important anymore, only the job and how well people would like the way I did it."

My sympathies were with Robert, and I said so, glad to support him. "When I was weeding the other day," I said, around sips of tea, "I left one little patch, because I was feeling compulsive too. Maybe the answer is to leave a little mess behind. That's hard for me." Robert and I smiled at each other, feeling close.

Jane leaned across the table, her strong hands precisely folded. She was on the attack. "I'm uncomfortable with this leaving of deliberate messes," Jane said. "You should always do the best job you can. Leaving messes seems like a cop-out." She was not in sync with my attempt to get out of the ego, and I was furious, wanting to punch her right in the snoot. But since punches and arguments were not in the curriculum of the retreat, I smiled tightly and let the gauntlet fly by.

Jane disliked me for all the right reasons. She knew me for what I was because she was that way too, and didn't much like it. I learned later that Jane had a twin, a married sister who was a successful mother and career woman. The two of them didn't get along, and I could see why. Whatever I did to call attention to myself, Jane would imitate. We were like those *doppelgängers*, doubles, in Poe's stories who end by murdering each other, only to find they have committed suicide. Odd, that the ego on a destructive kick winds up killing itself. R. D. Laing said the same thing of schizophrenics who construct a dead area between themselves and others, only to find their isolated egos crumbling to dust behind the very wall built to protect them. Jane and I were like that, sick with the disease of self-consciousness. If we had lived side by side in a primitive culture, scrubbing our family's wash on the same rock, we might have sung songs together, exchanged complaints about our husbands, and been friends. As it was, we were single, alien intellects, programmed by a competitive culture to put out each other's light.

At the end of the retreat, when Linda announced to the group that she had asked me to write a book about us all and was inviting volunteers to tell me their stories, Jane spoke up strongly against the project. "I've seen books like this," she said, "and they falsify the encounter with God just by putting it into words. Everything people have felt here would become fake, novelized out of shape. I wouldn't want any part of it."

"The book will happen if it's supposed to," was all I said in reply, feeling smug and just. "I didn't ask for it and won't push it. People will tell me their stories if they want to."

Later that evening Jane slipped a note under my door, apologizing for "hurting me." I wrote back and told her that I wasn't at all hurt, annoyed that she thought she'd scored. And so Jane and I squabbled away our retreat, intent on being Queen of the May, sad as orphaned children, who, they say, are very polite to their caretakers in the hope of getting favors.

Linda did what she could to discourage our competition, and it wasn't until the end of the retreat that she told me I was the only one of the group whom she had guided personally. She told me that at a time when I was having a crisis of self-confidence, sure that I had a soul so dull that even God could see nothing in it. Other people seemed to be at a high level, absorbed in their breath prayers, their work and their point-gazing. As always, I was looking around for distractions and finding them. Sometimes I would admire Robert's thick brown beard and brawny shoulders. Other times I would follow the kittens around the yard, getting them to jump at twigs and vines I dangled just above their flailing paws. My eyes always found something to do until I closed them.

These other people seemed very holy in comparison to me. Linda assured me that was not the case, that God was just as much with me as with them. In retrospect I think she was letting me know that she saw no differences, not because they weren't there, but because she was not looking at them. She was loving as God loves, without distinctions. Such a love made clear to me the words of Jesus: Love God, love your neighbor as yourself. That's all there is. You love not with the alienating passion of the egotist, but without regard for barriers between selves or between self and God, the way light loves matter and penetrates it.

Martin had told me his own theory about the nature of light, which he, like Linda, saw as the blood of the universe. Photons for him were like spirit for me. "Light is everywhere at once," Martin told me, after we had attended an astronomy lecture. "It's falling through the universe, falling through our empty bodies at a speed past belief. We only imagine the universe is a solid place, and we are solid, separate beings in it. That's because we're blind."

As he spoke, I closed my eyes, suddenly imagining the collapse of my own bodily walls and the spreading of what was left of me into streaming particles that took off through the universe like Martin's photons, sprung by the big bang.

Linda must have felt like this in those early days at the Center, open-armed to all the universe, which had her clutched kindly between two intergalactic, widely spread arms. (Those arms, light-years' worth of arms . . . look at a map of the galaxy.) So there Linda was, wandering around the Center, looking for wood to burn, swinging her arms in the direction of God, stars, light.

One day Jane spoke to us, at Linda's request, about the light mysticism of Meister Eckhart, the 13th century German mystic and philosopher on whom she had done her recent doctoral dissertation. As she spoke, I understood what had brought her to the Center. She read her paper to us in a deep, strong voice that bounced off the walls like a Valkyrie's. What she wanted to be was a virgin soul, unbroken by experience, going non-stop from womb to God, like St. Thérèse of Lisieux. Only by melting her driving ego down to nothing could she become empty as she wished to be. Like Meister Eckhart, she wanted to see other beings not as objects, but as self-same things, to be given their freedom, not to be pushed around. Eckhart's God that-is-not-yet was for Jane the "silent, unlimited, unimaginable light which is quietly one with itself." To shed her own darkness, to become that light, was all Jane wanted. She longed to plant her feet in the compost of the ordinary, growing whatever seeds and branches come naturally. Though Jane waded hip-deep in the words of philosophers and saints, tight in the throat for living water, she was sure that she proceeded from God, was united with God, even when she felt empty as any Arizona gulch. To find the hidden God it was necessary to clean the stable of her soul until she could kneel and eat off the floor. Jane cleaned and cleaned, but still the stable was not clean enough, and she kept mourning the silent, hidden God who eluded her relentless search.

About the time we heard of Meister Eckhart's hidden God, we were invited to go to St. Benoit-du-lac, a Benedictine monastery from where the Center got the white, delicate cheese we ate three times a day. If God were in hiding, here was where you could start looking for him, I remember thinking as our car, driven rather aggressively by young Father Paul, fresh from the empty roads of Brazil, pulled up to the tall iron gates. Linda had wanted me to go to confession here, but the English-speaking priest was too busy, and Father Paul had heard mine that morning. He had not believed I was as bad as I thought I was. It didn't please me to be considered such an ordinary sinner. Perhaps a cloistered monk would have given my sins due weight, or so I liked to think. One by one the white-robed senior monks came in, following the black-robed young ones. Their faces were mostly thin and wore faint smiles. They looked very much like the archaic Greek figures that line the hall of the Metropolitan Museum of Art, engraved with an expression of continual surprise at the flow of the world passing them by in their stillness, breaking around them like water on rocks in its way.

Hearing the monks sing Gregorian chant in French, the older, white-robed ones standing close in a circle like conspirators, their heads together, I lost my sense of the centuries, and was tossed back to the time when I was deep in the Middle Ages, more than a student of them, because knowledge was not the point of that enterprise. From the time I first heard of Carthusian hermits and the knights of the Grail, part of my life was lived in their company. They were my tribe, and with them I could forget about books or ideas, being a child the way I used to be, mindless and glad, as they were in my eyes.

What had first put me in touch with the church was an atheistic professor of medieval history at my university, who peered at his classes through bright, almost sightless eyes, using no notes to lecture from because he couldn't see to read them. When his youngest child was born, he told us, no one had been prepared for a girl, and a name was not handy for the baptism. The baby was premature, struggling to breathe, and for some reason he wanted it baptized before it died. Rushing into the hall at the hospital in search of a name, he asked the first nun he saw what she was called, and then ran back to the pediatrician, who was leaning over the infant, holding a tiny oxygen mask.

"Hilary," my professor gasped, glad he had found a good medieval name. "Call her Hilary."

The professor's little daughter lived after all, a monument to the faith that surfaces at the desperate times when we are most ourselves, a faith that still hung on in this brilliant, half-blind, wholly alcoholic man. He was responsible indirectly for my baptism at 21 as well as for Hilary's, for he was the one who first taught me about the Children's Crusade, the knights and ladies who joined the peasants to haul rocks for the Cathedral of Chartres, and the blessed fool who juggled before the Madonna's statue because he had no other gift.

Watching the monks of St. Benoit, I was back again in the medieval world of my professor, the rise and fall of the monophonic chant echoing around me. With these white-robed monks, head to head in their circle of music, the West dropped a thousand years of history, and as I heard them, tasting the communion wafer pressed by the priest so hard I could feel the circumference of it, tears started down my face, tears for the broken circle of my own age, for my own divided mind, through whose cracks all the juices had run out, leaving me dry. Now I knew why Gregorian chant had always struck me as happy and sad at the same time—the music mourned the death of the old man and celebrated the birth of the new one. Maybe a sperm feels this sort of death when he bumps into an egg and starts growing as a new, fused self, more than he was, less than he will someday be. When we are downcast, we should remember that out of billions, we are the sperm that made it. Anyway, what was dying in me and being mourned by the monks was something I no longer wanted. The tears felt good. A wound which I didn't know I had was being healed. That most people were walking wounded, just as I was, had not seemed real to me until now, listening to the monks' chant, and when later that day Peter explained how this wound kept us from loving, I listened as if my life depended on it, which in a way it did.

"*The Cloud of Unknowing* says your ego is the real barrier between you and God," Peter told us, as he set up the tape recorder for the usual afternoon lecture. "Some methods of meditation taught today get rid of ego-consciousness through self-hypnosis. That's not our way here. We break the walls down with love, for by loving we do what God does and become like him. This love is what Jesus asked of us when he said, 'Be perfect even as your Father in heaven is perfect.' Anyone here have a question? There's a lot to ask about 'perfect.' "

Jane was listening intently, as always.

"Isn't the difference between contemplation and self-hypnosis really that self-hypnosis restricts our consciousness and that contemplation expands it?" she asked.

Stroking his short curly beard, Peter nodded. "That's what Menninger says on this tape. The ego spends a lot of time censoring and distorting reality, limiting it to what our tiny selves can understand. Wordless prayer does the opposite—it gets us out of the way so God can fill us up with love. We become what we know, Who we know." He switched on the tape and sat down to eat.

Menninger began with a tale of two men who saw an orange in the market. They had never seen an orange before and wanted to know all they could about it. One man went to the library and did research on oranges until he knew all about their nutritive elements, the history of their cultivation, and the various types available, depending on whether you want juice or sections to eat by hand. The other man simply took the orange and ate it. Which of them really knew best what an orange is?

The parable struck home to me especially hard, since always I had studied life, in particular the life of the past, rather than living it directly. I had done what many theologians had done with prayer—compile and study the insights gained by the saints after prayer with the hope that by analyzing their results we will feel as if we have prayed too. But we bring ourselves into the scene and our busy intellects arrange the facts their own way, drawing their own conclusions. It's like those exhausting vacations, where we come back more frantic than when we left. The problem with most vacations is that *we* go along, chattering, planning, grabbing everything in sight, or trying to. How different such a vacation is from a simple honeymoon by a hidden lake in the woods with someone you love more than you love yourself.

Your mind is filled with the presence of the other, as the contemplative's mind is filled with God. Because God is measureless, so is love. (I remember that Martin asked me once what Christians believe God is, and I read him the words of 1 John: "Anyone who fails to love can never have known God, because God is love.") St. Bernard of Clairvaux wrote in the 12th century that you must be moderate in all but love, and that anyone who contemplates can't err in this respect, unless he's some kind of idiot who's *always* wrong.

At this point in the tape, I began to laugh, shaking silently, my hand pressed over my mouth. Brother Jonathan's eye caught mine and he turned red, panting and giggling, holding his plump sides as if they hurt. The others tried to look at their plates and concentrate on the breath prayers but soon even Sister Anna was holding her napkin over her mouth, her shoulders quivering, and frail old Michael slapped his thigh, laughing out loud, not caring who heard. I had to rush outside and sit on a bench under the pine tree before I could stop. Therese came out too, and sat beside me, hiccupping and wiping her eyes.

"It's always like this halfway through retreats," she whispered. "Everybody breaks up."

Like children, I thought, nodding. I hadn't laughed so hard since I was in grade school and had to be sent from the room because my unstoppable giggling infected all the others. Just as a child often can't stop laughing or crying once he starts, so we on our retreat were at the mercy of our long-buried child selves which had been unearthed in silent prayer and solitude, where they still were.

It was the child in us who was capable of faith and love, as it was capable of spontaneous laughter and tears. The child is filled up by the moment and takes no thought of what will happen next. A baby who reaches out his arms for his mother has no scheme in mind. He isn't trying to use or manipulate her. He *is* his need, his love, and is not separate from it. The adult has learned to split himself from his need and consequently falls into using what he calls "love" to control others and get pleasure from them without regard for their interests. "Love is the good of the other," Augustine wrote in the fourth century, and that truth has not changed. And because physical love, split as it is from feelings, is such a contemporary obsession, Peter and Linda felt they must stress sexuality as a divine, creative force which issues at its highest in loving prayer, a perfect union of mind and body with God.

Toward the middle of the second week, when we had become familiar with every line, bump and variation in color of our brown squares, we were given a new exercise to do while point-gazing—the Consecration of Sexual Energies, in which sex was not repressed, but transformed into Christ's own love. We all sat around the living room, crowded cozily on the flowered sofas or sitting in rows on the picnic benches at the table, and Peter gave us a little talk on Christian sex, while Sister Anna blushed and Jonathan leaned over to give her a hug, as he often did, knowing from her tight mouth how much she needed it. At first there was some embarrassed laughter and a few jokes. We were like kids in a locker room, being lectured by the coach. Robert the seminarian was listening with special intensity, leaning forward a little, and I remembered how he had confessed on the first day of the retreat that he suffered from his sexuality.

Linda took over the discussion halfway through, and there was one thing she was especially clear and frank about, perhaps because she had been a married woman and a mother for so long—the role of the body in prayer. The body was to be treated as a loved partner in the enterprise of encountering God, not starved, denied its legitimate needs, made to suffer, or blamed as the source of sin.

For Linda and Peter, sexuality was another name for creative energy, and a model for the coming together of God and man in love. In the Song of Songs and the words of Christ about his husbandly love for his church, Linda found her scriptural authority. The teaching of the church on the sacrament of marriage, equal in power and validity to the sacrament of ordination, was another support for her appreciation of the body as a vessel of grace. Above all, Linda believed in the Incarnation as a baptism of the body, everyone's body. What God had declared sacred enough to be his temple was sacred enough to be ours.

"But doesn't the church teach that virginity is better than marriage?" Sister Anna looked down at her lap, but she spoke firmly, sure of her ground, perhaps wanting to be sure of the rightness of her choice. Later I learned that only in escaping from family life had Anna been able to find sanity and safety.

Better or worse had no meaning here, Linda gently pointed out. In sexual love, the lover can see not only the beloved, but God who is the ground of the beloved's being and of his or her own. The creative energies of our own bodies and the creative love of God himself converge and neither we nor he are separate in that moment.

Having guarded my children carefully against the sensual lyrics of popular songs and the influence of permissively raised friends, I was suspicious of this celebration of the body and wondered if it were just another way of watering down the hard life of discipline and sensory deprivation that masters of all spiritual traditions teach is necessary for contemplation. Instant mysticism without sacrifice or struggle had after all become commonplace through drugs, and transcendental meditation offered almost as dramatic a route to ecstasy. So I wondered if Linda's way were not simply another easy spiritual high.

But I was mistaken if I thought that sexuality in Linda's view could simply continue to pour out at the mindless, generative level and remain independent of the transformation going on in the rest of the human being under the influence of the Holy Spirit. Like prayer, speech and work, sexual energies were to be baptized into the kingdom of God. They were not repressed, as I had dutifully tried to do, developing psoriasis and allergies along the way, nor to be exalted as an end in themselves, but used as a sort of electric current on which the whole mind tuned into nature and God.

Robert had been listening intently, his sturdy arms wrapped tightly around the pillow in his lap. "So what you're saying is that sex isn't bad? We don't have to clamp a manhole cover down tight on our physical feelings?" He was smiling and wiped a hand across his mouth as if afraid we would see the smile.

Jane jumped into the pause before Peter answered. Peter thought before he spoke, while Jane, like the teacher she was, thought on her feet.

"Careful," she said. "Make no mistake here. Anybody who wants to be celibate and has a strong sex urge is going to have to sit on it a lot. I know."

She probably did. Jane was a fiery type, all right, and must have sat on a lot of urges in her years as a nun.

She folded her hands firmly on her lap. "No use pretending it's easy or doesn't hurt. For some of us, it hurts more than anything."

Father Paul looked up mildly from the Christmas card he was putting together. "Everything hurts when it's forced," he said in his light young voice. "Only love makes it easy. Jesus said that his burden was light enough for us to bear it. Love makes it easy. Only love."

"But how? How?" Robert burst out. "I do love God. How can I turn one kind of love into the other? Physical love into love of God? That's what I really want to know. Can it be done? If not, I might as well quit right now." He hugged his pillow, buried his face in it, and subsided.

"Will power," Jane said kindly, putting her hand on his shoulder like a wise veteran comforting a young recruit in the trenches. "Will power and grace. It's been done before."

"Love too," Peter said, standing up and walking over to the window. "Love doesn't force, love creates something new." He turned back to us. "What you're doing here, I think, is turning your sexual urges into sacred love. God gave you desire and raw energy to make new life. The desire is not evil, but is from God. Also from God is the call to give birth to your new self, and to others, not by a physical act, but by the Spirit. Being born again, Jesus called it. With practice we will teach you what we know about it. Anyone can learn to raise his sexual energies out of his lower body."

"But isn't sex just totally different from anything spiritual?" Sister Anna insisted, her voice low but insistent. "Isn't that why we give it up, in order to have God? How can we have both?"

"It's not the sex that gets between God and us," old Michael said, his pale blue eyes looking watery all of a sudden. I remembered hearing that he had recently lost his wife and missed her very much. "It's wanting to use someone else, wanting power over them. Sex is the least of it. The sex is healthy, anyway. Love of power isn't healthy at all."

"Sex can be a way of owning somebody, making them do what you want," Peter said, nodding in agreement, "or it can be a way of expressing love. Here we're talking about expressing love, not using raw energy. The love comes from God and returns to God. It doesn't get stuck somewhere in between."

"In the ego," Alison suddenly said in a loud voice, then added in a softer, embarrassed tone, "it usually gets stuck in the ego."

Peter smiled at her and she looked down, examining her bitten nails., "It might not get stuck," he said. "It might just start flowing upwards, not out of our lower body. And if it reversed itself and went up, where would it go?"

"To the heart." Father Paul put his Christmas cards on the shelf. "Straight to the heart." He began to walk back and forth in front of the window like Peter, looking out whenever he passed. "And we would feel such a strong pull toward up that it would be like having children with God, and taking care of them."

I remembered that Paul was a missionary and had given birth to souls in his way. Always before, I had felt sorry for people who had not had children out of their own bodies. Looking at Paul's face, insistent and glad, I didn't feel sorry for him now.

"Don't separate the desire of your bodies from the desire of your hearts," Peter was saying. "The same love is in both, given by God, beginning and ending in him. We're only antennae, transmitters of the love that moves the stars and grows a baby in the body of a woman. Every sexual act is a potential incarnation and every act of spiritual love is an incarnation too, a form of spiritual energy. No difference. What we will do here is to bring the energy we call sex into your heart, where it will become the creative life of God in you. Whether you're celibate or married doesn't matter. What matters is that you bring all your energy, all your desire, up into your hearts and offer it to God, offer it to other people in an act of love."

8 THE STORY OF ROBERT

My brothers, remember that you have been
called to live in freedom—but not a freedom
that gives free rein to the flesh. Out of love,
place yourselves at one another's service. The
whole law has found its fulfillment in this one
saying: "You shall love your neighbor as
yourself."

Galatians 5:13-15

Robert was a giant of a man, built like an oak tree, with a heavy beard and curling dark hair all over his arms, legs, and chest. His features were strong and regular, his smile quick and contagious. Robert looked so alive that other people in the room seemed pallid and frail by contrast, like invalids in the presence of an athlete. When Peter had first seen this young man walk through the door, he remembered dreaming about him the night before. In his dream, a centaur with a face and upper body that Peter now recognized as Robert's, was unhappily trying to wash his lower, animal half. Peter often had a dream before retreats in which the most deeply wounded and needy of the retreatants was made known to him. This time, the needy one was Robert.

No less likely candidate for pity could be imagined, for Robert was blessed with beauty, health and a kind heart. Everyone loved him. But Robert always needed more love than he got, and his need was quietly driving him crazy.

"Father, we know that your life has no end and that all things are open and clear to you," Peter prayed aloud. "Give us your powerful light so that we will know your law of love and try to live it with chaste hearts and chaste bodies and chaste minds now and always, forever and ever, through Christ our Lord."

Robert remembered standing before the communion rail
as a young child, saying "I love you, Jesus," the crucifix filling his eyes and a mysterious joyful energy filling his heart.
The kid next to him nudged him in the ribs, whispering, "It's
time to sit down now. What's the matter with you?" Robert
turned red, quick as always to think he had done the wrong
thing, and sat with the others. The moments with Jesus had
passed too fast, and he was back in the real world, regretting
his loss, remembering his sins. He stirred uneasily in the pew,
hoping the priest who looked so sternly down at him could
not read his thoughts. For even then, at seven, Robert could
not regard himself as chaste. Only he knew what his sins
were, but he always feared others might know too. It was
hard to be chaste, to keep his mind pure, when everywhere
he looked there were pictures of women lounging in bikinis,
seductively inviting men to try the product they advertised.
A boy would have to walk around all day with his eyes
closed not to be infected with the culture's sexual obsession.
Some boys managed by turning it into a joke, but Robert's
fertile mind created elaborate fantasies out of the uncon-
trollable surgings in his body and tormented him beyond
bearing.

"The Western world doesn't leave much room for the
Christian sacramental view of sex," Peter went on. "Only images of profane sexuality are put before us. In the Tantric
tradition, the figure of the woman was divine, an avenue to
God. Even here in the West, during the Middle Ages, we had
the Madonna, whose feminine nature mothered souls. But in
our own time, we have nothing except the girl on the
billboard or movie marquee who is all body, the avenue not
to God but to some mindless, temporary thrill. Sex has
become a fix, like a shot of heroin or a sniff of cocaine. For
the Christian, it cannot be so, because the body is the temple
of the Holy Spirit, and the love expressed between man and
woman is in fact the love of God himself. St. John of the
Cross thought of the soul as the bride of Christ, and saw the

love between the soul and God as the ultimate destination of the human love that begins in the body. Only in Christ can that love be channeled upward into the heart and made divine. Only then does it stop exploiting the other person as an object, and become what Jesus meant by love."

Robert nodded his head at Peter's words, thinking that if a man could love like that, he would no longer be compelled to use his body in ways that left him drained and despairing. A man whose body belonged to God was free. Robert had always wanted that freedom. Sexual fantasies and sexual acts left him dissatisfied, wanting more than ever the simple, perfect love he had felt in moments of prayer like those before the communion rail. As a high school sophomore, Robert read the New Testament through for the first time, astonished at the love of Christ for the people around him. The love of Christ made him cry with joy because he knew it was for him too. He began again to think of the priesthood, for the first time since he was a child. If he could pour all the desire of his body into love for Jesus, he knew he could be a priest. But he would need help in controlling the energies that rolled through him and the fantasies that pulled his mind every which way.

When Peter spoke of channeling sexual desire into the heart, where it would be consecrated to God's use, Robert understood. He had entered a New York seminary at 18, moved by a strong urge to live a life of service. His study at the seminary was coordinated with a B.S. in human services from a secular university. These years were busy with studies, community life at the seminary, apostolic work and a ministry to youth during the summers. Gradually Robert felt his faith grow up. He became more certain that Jesus was at the center of his life; he knew this not with his head but with his heart. At the same time, a struggle was beginning in him which would test both his faith and his priesthood. It was this struggle which led him to the Thomas Merton Center. Like Isaiah, he felt God was saying to him, "Yes, I am making a road in the wilderness, paths in the wilds." Robert had come to this desert in order to find his way out of that other desert in which his desires had left him stranded and dry.

Now that he was a full-grown man, Robert had learned that the compulsive search for physical love was only a symptom of a deeper sickness: his inability to love himself. Even God, he felt, could not love someone as corrupt as he was. In his earlier years he had worked to earn love by doing every task perfectly and by pleasing everyone around him. If only he could seem good enough, perhaps people would give him the love they would surely deny him if they knew how bad he really was. In his need for love, he would cling to those who gave it to him until his demands made them grow cold and distant. Then he would feel despair again, suffering from the old fear that he was no good. More than once, close relationships between Robert and those he loved had cracked when he put on too much pressure. The people he loved weren't God, and when he wanted an absolute love, they had only human love to offer.

The fever that had burned in him as long as he could remember peaked and broke in the spring before he came to the Center. At that time, Robert was deep in a relationship with a young woman which seemed to be going the way of all the others. Again he was driven by need, again he was using another person to fill that need. On Palm Sunday, hearing the words from the Passion of St. Matthew, the denial of Christ by Peter, "I do not know the man," Robert realized he had not known or loved himself, because his sexuality seemed to him an overwhelming evil. He had taken from others and never given, denying what he had received. Over the next few weeks, all his shame and grief began to pour out of him in tears that felt like a bath for his soul.

Soon afterward, a faculty member at the seminary told him about the Center. Robert determined to go there for an immersion of his body, mind and spirit in prayer. He was more and more sure that only in God would he find his freedom and his rest. Certainly he wasn't finding rest in sexual love. Once at the Center, he took as his breath prayer, "Lord Jesus, heal me deeply," for he felt only God could find and cure the wound he had made in his own soul. Would he commit himself to the celibate life for good, or would he continue to search for love in this world? He asked Peter for a night in the hermitage, the little shack in the woods, where he might pray alone and hear God's will for him.

Once in the hermitage with his bag of bread and fruit and the inevitable Benedictine cheese, Robert settled into solitude. As he did his usual evening sitting, alone in the woods, he was aware that distractions were screaming for attention as usual, but that his prayer was quiet despite them. For a little while after his sitting, he rested on the bed, saying his breath prayer, asking to be healed as he had hoped since his arrival at the Center. At once he felt a strong urge to practice the Consecration of Sexual Energies. As Peter had taught him to do, he began to picture a geyser moving up toward his heart, and he felt the presence of God rising through him like living water. His while body tingled in answer, and waves of warmth rolled through it. He asked God to consecrate him as a channel of this divine, life-giving energy so that he might love others as God loves them. The decision was made. He would be a priest.

When he returned to the farmhouse, Robert prepared for the Prayer of Listening session before dinner by reading John 7:37-38: "In the last day, the great day of the feast, Jesus stood and cried, saying, if any man thirst, let him come unto me and drink. He that believes in me, as the scriptures have said, out of his heart shall flow rivers of living water." Robert now knew he was a channel for the grace of God, a way for God's love to reach the world. He looked around at everyone in the room with new eyes. The women no longer made him think erotic thoughts, but were sacred. Everyone was sacred. He blessed them all silently, filled with love. At the very moment he was giving all he had, he saw how utterly poor he was without God, and he suddenly felt God's presence at his heart's core. He was leaning on the body of God, like St. John on Christ's breast at the Last Supper. Not a word was said, but he was being fed so much love that he could say afterward only "beautiful, beautiful, beautiful!" Never had he been given to in such a way. Never would he look for love from any other source. His weaknesses, anxieties and fantasies would not disappear overnight, maybe not over a lifetime, he knew, but now he could accept them as a part of himself, placed in God's hands like the rest of him. In the past, he realized, he had almost enjoyed the torment he inflicted on himself. But the great scenario in which he, the suffering hero, had starred was over. The actor was gone, and in his place was a new man, at peace and healed. Once he had thought God was some strange, faraway being, but now God was next to him, with him, within him, giving him what he needed. As Robert put it in his journal, "I have found the Heart of Hearts in His."

9 WORK AS PRAYER

"As long as the day lasts I must carry out the
work of the one who sent me; the night will
soon be here when no man can work. As long
as I am in the world, I am the light of the
world."

John 9:4-5

Robert had begun his stay at the Center working furiously hard, harder than anyone else, scraping and painting the
second story of the house, bare-chested and sweating in the
bright sunlight. He was applying his whole self to his labor,
ending only at the last minute, when the bell rang for prayer,
as if he regretted having to leave the active sphere for the one
where he was less at home. Often he would exhaust himself
so thoroughly that he would fall asleep during the sitting,
with his head on his chest, snoring so loudly that Brother
Jonathan would have to lean over and jostle him awake.
Robert seemed to be trying to burn up his fierce energy, using
work to distract his body from its craving for sex. It took him
several weeks at the Center to understand that all energy was
a single energy, and that prayer was only a continuation of
work, as the hand is of the arm. The body that prays is the
same body that works.

Because action and contemplation appear to us as
separate activities, we forget that the person doing both is
one person, unifying whatever he does simply by being what
is. Children have not yet forgotten. When my children were
small, we discovered an ant war going on in front of our
house, and spent the afternoon squatting on the sidewalk like
Olympians watching the progress of this epic battle between
red and black. Over the hours, red ants dragged away the big
black corpses to eat and black ants fell back to a new and

more defensible line, behind a long, grass-filled crack. No time seemed to pass. The scale of the ants was such that a human hundred years' war was being fought in a few hours. We onlookers were not part of their cosmos or cut to their measure, and so, patient as God, we watched heroes fall, wounded comrades borne away, and a civilization die. When the blacks had been defeated, I looked up and saw the sun was setting. The children began to whine with hunger that they hadn't felt till they came back to themselves. We had all come back and were wearing different heads again. For a little while we had been caught up in a new world, had no more awareness of false selves, and were playing no games with our own images.

It was all very well, I began to understand the desire to win; but whenever you win, someone else loses. I thought painfully of my mortal combat with Jane. All my life I had been winning, not seeing the bodies of the losers on the field, my own among them. My head was all I needed, so the body was not missed.

Like any thoroughly conditioned, well-adjusted modern person, I acted on the belief that the highest good was the control and use of my world. The intrusions of reality—laundry, dust, the messes made by human beings as they conduct their daily business—all insulted me with their claims to my attention. As I dealt with them, I held my nose, sleepwalked where possible, and only went through motions, never appreciating what I was having while I was having it. What could have caused such a pathological impatience with the moment at hand? Perhaps I dimly saw that the physical, ordinary world I wanted to run in fact belongs to no one but God.

Because it was clear to me that the real world could not be controlled absolutely, I learned to live in my imagination, the only place where I could play god. It was in that world I lived exclusively, hating whatever forced me out of it. Above all I hated cooking and cleaning, which reminded me that I was no more than a servant in my own house. So all those housekeeping years passed, teaching me nothing, or rather they moved ahead, slowly as geologic ages in which mountain ranges rise and fall.

In the course of my life as a young mother one person helped me to understand that work could be an easy yoke, a burden borne lightly. She was a woman who worked as a maid in rich people's houses, and owned, with her laborer-husband, the two-family Detroit house in which my husband and I were raising our small children. Our hope was to begin the children's lives in a multiracial neighborhood so they would learn a sympathy for black people which children in a lily-white suburb rarely do. Grace's husband Bill, a smart, angry, middle-aged man, had dropped out of college and gone to work in Ford's steel plant during the Depression. He was like me, hating the physical world which got in his way, tripping him every time he took a step. Bill would sit on the porch above ours during his weekends, drink raw whiskey and read the encyclopedia. My husband was studying for his Ph.D. exam and Bill loved to confound him with hard questions.

"When did Shelley and Lord Bryon (which was how he insisted Byron's name was pronounced) live together at Lake Geneva?" he called over the railing, his white smile broad with delight at knowing what he knew. When my husband couldn't answer, Bill would crow and slap his knee. "White boy, if you ever goin' pass that exam, you better know the facts. 1816, boy. The summer of 1816."

Bill would sit and talk to me in the tiny back yard while I played with the children, arguing about literature which he loved and describing the furnace room of the steel mill which he hated. "I got no pleasure in that place," he said. "Man, it hot. Like 120 degrees in there. My brain start to boil and I hate the man who gives me coal to shovel like I hate the fire I shovels it into. Like living in hell, is that bitter place." Bill was a man of imagination and like me lived in his head, where he could run things. He adored his plump, laughing wife, but Grace's Christian acceptance of their lot made him sick with anger. "She the best woman that lives," he whispered to me one day, "but she a *square*." He smiled his white smile and made his thumbs and forefingers into a square through which he peered at me with one bloodshot, malevolent eye. "You and I know that nothin' is the way Grace see it." So Bill drank, brooded and kicked against the traces.

Meanwhile Grace worked and lived without thought, her every word and action so heavy with love that she had to move slowly, like an astronaut on Jupiter or a priest celebrating Mass. One night, after a crash and screaming from across the alley, I heard a sobbing woman, just beaten by her husband, run to our back door. All the way up the stairs, Grace was talking to her. "You just come right on in, honey. No one goin' hurt you now." Grace loved everyone the way she loved Jesus, and was everyone's mother, perhaps beause she had no children of her own. As she cleaned her house, I would hear her singing gospel hymns in her big deep voice, and imagined that she sang the same songs with the same joyful passion when she scrubbed the floors of the rich folks across the river in Grosse Pointe.

Grace loved children, and when my third baby was born, begged to borrow him from time to time. As she sat rocking him, cradling him next to her big breasts, such an expression would come over her broad, damp face that I had to turn away, ashamed that not even my own child could evoke in me what a stranger's child did in this woman. She invited her women's bible group over one day and asked me if I would bring the baby up for a little while. When I came back for him, the women were passing him around, their voices soft as lullabies, saying, "Lord, he white. You ever see anything white as that?" Grace took him back from them and handed him over, looking me deeply in the eyes. "This a lamb of God," she said. "You got a lamb of God in your

arms." That particular child has always been blessed and protected, perhaps because in his infancy he had been held and
loved by a saint.

Like Grace, Linda believed the world was not a bad
place and that the work done in it was a sacrament, not a
grim duty. Linda told us so during one of her brief afternoon
talks as we sat around the living room, relieved at the sound
of any human voice, and at this one in particular, low, strong
and sure. She had read Teilhard de Chardin and taken in his
vision of the world as the body of God, of matter as sacred,
not separate from us. The universe began without form, she
said, and God worked on it. This was the first labor and from
it came, in the course of the ages, a consciousness, ours,
through which God could know his own creation as inseparable from himself, like a mother tied to her just-born
child by a cord full of blood. "Work is creative, like play,"
she told us, "and it can't be forced without becoming split
from you. It isn't separate, but comes from you, out of your
prayer, because you want it. You can't make yourself work
creatively any more than you can make yourself play.
Remember you are in sacred time. Whatever you do to shape
the world is a prayer. You have the whole world in both
hands. Try not to work with any thought of results. The
fruits will come by themselves, but for us, there's just the
work. Nothing but the work."

Peter spoke after his wife had finished. He was cautious
in presenting work to us. Probably a lot of retreatants, asked
to paint the house or weed the garden, had complained of being exploited. They had paid for a vacation and here they
were doing slave labor on someone else's farm. The world
outside the Center had taught us well: Get what you pay for
and let no one take advantage of you.

"We know that many of you come from high-stress
situations," Peter said, warming his hands around the teacup,
maybe thinking of Michael, the ex-alcoholic, heart attack patient. "If you need rest, say so. If the work helps you to make

a bridge between your prayer and the world you live in, ask for more of it. Don't split your work from God. The big thing is to think of the work itself as prayer. That's what it is. Say the breath prayer as you work. It will help keep your mind on your business. Never let go of that business. It's your Father's, not just yours."

Sister Anna, the shy Canadian, knew the truth of what Peter had said to us. Her two deepest experiences during the retreat came not in chapel but while scrubbing the floor and bringing groceries out of the store in town. Once I heard her whisper to Father Paul, the blond young priest, that she had never seen lights or visions. "Neither have I," Father Paul replied. "I just make the oatmeal around here." Yet the two of them had the most solid practice, the strongest tenacity, of any retreatants at the Center. For them both, the way they loved God was through their vocation, which became in their lives no different from their prayer. It was not that they worked instead of praying, but that their prayer and their work had become one thing, inseparable from what they were at their hearts' core, where they knew God.

What we had to learn at the Center was that our work was no more separate from our prayer than God was from the world he made and kept alive. This saying was a hard one for me, since I regarded prayer as my legitimate way to get out of work, on the same order as illness, but more dignified. I would much have preferred to be saved by faith rather than by good works, and like Luther had always felt comforted by the words, "The just shall be saved by faith." Of course, I never asked myself what being just meant, for I guessed that it involved working hard. Sitting in a chapel, with the sun's rays slanting through the window and edging the rim of my gold circle with light, it was easy to blame the post-Reformation church for cautiously stressing good works. The church was fearful that ecstatic prayer might carry people away into pride or anarchy. They might forget to work and serve humbly, want only to fly away and be at rest.

A tape was played for us one day at dinner which recounted for us the flowering of medieval mysticism and its ending in the private revelations of individuals who set up faiths of their own. Modern Christians, the voice on the tape explained, were taught to apply themselves to good works only, leaving communion with God to a handful of ascetics. Even the Ignatian *Spiritual Exercises*, meant to teach people how to pray, concentrated on discursive prayer, controlled by words, images and an official guide. When St. John of the Cross had his visions in the 16th century, he was imprisoned for months in a latrine and beaten every day. If he hadn't died first, he would have been prosecuted by the Inquisition for his belief that God is living in us and that we can know him as he is.

From this fear of the Counter-Reformation church that individuals would get what Dostoevsky's skeptics called "religious mania" and go stampeding off to set up little groups of their own came the fear of contemplation itself, and the intent of church authorities to keep the faithful in line, paying their money, doing their penances and leaving real prayer to a few saints who would save the world by proxy. I remember that at the end of this pedantic tape, full of dogma and references to the Fathers of the church, we had begun to slump in our chairs, our eyes glazing over, like those of my students when I become possessed by an idea and harangue them about the godless follies of the French Enlightenment. Brother Jonathan, whose tolerance for boredom was even lower than mine, rolled his eyes as the faint, sepulchral academic voice of the speaker wound down on the machine. As it faded altogether, Brother Jonathan whispered confidentially to us all, "He died." Even correct Sister Anna laughed until her eyes ran.

We didn't take too well to historical lectures, all of us being there because we had heard too many lectures and got too little from them. We were at the Center to learn how to live our lives, how to unify our prayer with our work, and words weren't much help. What we needed was *practice*, the day-to-day incarnation of the carpenter-Christ who spent 30 years in his mother's house, silent, with hands that never stopped working.

Father Paul, the missionary priest from Brazil, wanted his work to be a sacred dance, inseparable from his own prayer. For a long time he had been a divided man and he had come to the Center to learn how he could both be what he was and do his work. Nothing in the modern world taught him that his integration was possible. Men were the specialized animals, skilled at analysis and technology, no longer whole. He was beginning to resign himself to being two men, the one who worked and the one who prayed.

10 THE STORY OF PAUL

"At least believe in the work that I do; then
you will know for sure that the Father is in
me and I am in the Father."

John 10:38

Paul Duval sat on the low, slanted Japanese meditation
bench which he had made himself, and faced the altar. He
was wondering why he was here at the Center instead of in a
parish or mission field like other priests. He had begun like
them, but somewhere along the line had found that
priesthood without prayer was not enough for him. He was
only 29, but had already spent six years trying every form of
religious life, from Benedictine monasticism to missionary
work in the Brazilian jungles. His long blond hair framed a
sturdily handsome face, with skin as smooth as an altar
boy's, deeply tanned by days tending the Center's gardens
and grounds. He focused his large, earth-colored eyes on the
monstrance, determined to keep his mind on the business at
hand, which was reviewing his past, following God's foot-
prints in his life. Paul liked to talk, and when no one was
there to talk to, his mind jumped and danced by itself, a party of one. He needed inner silence. Ever since he entered the
seminary, he had sought silence, but had not found it.

His anti-clerical French Canadian family had never encouraged Paul to think the priesthood offered instant sanctity
or guaranteed the beatific vision in this life. The family had
been mad at Paul when he became a priest, and gave him up
as hopeless when he volunteered for the missions in Brazil. Of
the seven Duval children, he was the only one to be religious.
Though his mother and grandmother had occasional bursts
of fervor, no one in his family understood when he said he
wanted to search for God. Even before he could read, Paul

used to sit on the floor staring at pictures of Noah and the flood in the family Bible, his heart full of pity and terror at the convulsed limbs sticking out of the water in appeal to Noah, who stood safe, dry and patriarchally stern at the railing of the ark. Paul's early religious life was lived in the golden time of the fifties, when no one asked questions about what you were really trying to do when you prayed and everyone practiced his faith with a sort of innocent enthusiasm. Paul was a warm, emotional man, and had been no different as a child. He went to Mass like the others, and on Good Fridays wept over Jesus' falling for the third time, but that was all.

When the revolution of the sixties went into high gear, Paul was entering high school, and his growing to physical maturity coincided with the coming of the new Mass and its colloquial English, guitars and turned-around altar. Paul continued to go to Mass out of habit, but his heart wasn't in it. The sentiment that moved him in his childhood to cry on Good Fridays no longer moved him, and he seldom prayed anymore. As an adolescent, Paul withdrew into himself, except for the hours spent with a small group of friends. Living as they did in rural Michigan, the boys escaped the drug and sex craze of the era. They played football and joined the debating team. Their few rebellions were mild: drinking a six-pack together, or necking with girls in the graveyard. At church, Paul was a reluctant member of a youth group which featured the right-on Eucharist. One night only four people showed up to bake the communion bread, and Paul was one of them. As the priest worked and prayed with the teenagers, Paul was suddenly struck by the sense that the five were no longer a group, but one and the same, all moved by a joy that floated Paul home at the end of the evening. "If a priest can do that for people," he thought, "if a priest can make them feel they matter and are not alone, then I want to be a priest." Paul was uncertain about whether or not he was good enough to be a priest. Maybe he would just be a brother.

At Michigan State University, Paul decided on a teaching career, studying Russian and French. He avoided those students who had by now caught up with the rest of the country, majoring in alcohol, drugs and sex, preferring to pour his own energies into daily Mass, study and the anti-war movement. His religion was the formal, traditional kind he remembered from the fifties; his social conscience, however, was up to date. He had become a sophisticated adult in political and social affairs but was still a child in spiritual matters.

Not until Paul entered the Missionhurst Seminary after two years of college, did his faith grow up. At first he was confused and shocked when his theology professors demolished his simple notions of who God was and how he wished to be worshiped. The rector told his seminarians that they must start "listening to God." Paul had no idea what the rector meant. No one ever explained mental prayer in the seminary until Paul went on a seven-day retreat at the end of the first year. At that time he was given the Ignatian exercises, but the great contemplatives like St. Teresa of Avila and St. John of the Cross were still unknown to him. When Paul prayed, he talked to himself about himself. If God were in on this conversation, he never made his presence known. What did it mean to "listen to God"? Paul began to read every spiritual book he could get his hands on. By the time he had finished his novitiate, he was experiencing periods of stillness when the words in his head would stop during the time prescribed for discursive prayer. The urge came over him to join a contemplative community, and he asked permission to go to the Thomas Merton Center, about which he had read in the *National Catholic Reporter*. His superiors said no. "We're missionaries," they told Paul. "Contemplation is not a charism of our order." So he asked to make a retreat at a Benedictine abbey in northern New York State for a summer volunteer program. This time permission was granted.

At the monastery he cleaned pig sties, planted gardens and biked four miles for Mass before dawn. From 5:30 to eight in the morning, Paul was free to pray alone. The abbot asked him one day how he was enjoying his visit, and Paul answered that he loved the silence. The abbot laughed. "And we think it's so damned noisy around here," he said. But the monastery was offering Paul the first chance in his life to experience prolonged periods of silence. He often began his meditation with a reading from the poetry of Catherine de Vinck. As the sun rose over the Adirondacks, he would sit at his window, remembering the words he had just read:

> "Lord," I say
> I am plucked out
> lifted into soundless space.
> The tongue tries further speech;
> The mind furiously looks
> for clipped bits of phrases
> but words are shot down. . . .
> What was it that I sought?
> A pure language, a way
> of speaking the truth
> nothing but the truth.
>
> Now silence is held to my lips
> a hot coal, a perfect answer.

And Paul would lay Catherine's book aside, wanting no more words, not even those. Despite his deep immersion in the monastic life, he still felt that he had not come close to finding God. Something was in the way.

In 1961, Paul's father had died from stomach cancer. At the time, Paul expressed little of his grief and none of his anger. Now he remembered how cancer patients were told it was all right to be mad at God for what was happening. "God can take it," said one of the supervisors when Paul was working briefly in a cancer ward. On the anniversary of his father's death, while walking down a country road near the monastery, Paul suddenly felt the old, long-stopped rage at his father's suffering begin to pour out of him. He stood still on the road and wept, then cried out to God, "I hate your guts." As the childish words came, so did an awareness of his own foolish expectation that God would obey him, indulge him as his father once had. A peace spread into his work, into his solitary prayer. Paul was no longer angry with God; nothing stood between them.

More and more he was unhappy with the community he lived in. His prayer life was not shared with others or supported by them. When he visited the mission in Haiti, he saw that the priests were basically social workers. Prayer was at the edges of their lives, hardly noticed in the flood of sorrowing, hungry people that poured through the doors of the mission house.

Paul too was hungry. Every book he could find on prayer and meditation he ate up, feeling he was in imminent danger of death from spiritual malnutrition. He wanted to go into the wilderness but held back, caught up in the social service gospel of the sixties. After his ordination he worked in a Michigan parish, moving from job to unending job in his own community, two nearby ones, and the local Veterans hospital. He smiled at people often until he realized that whenever he smiled, they would suck him into their lives, taking the last moments of the day he might have had for prayer. He walked around grimly, looking at the ground, afraid even to meet anyone's eyes for fear he would be trapped again. "It's my time versus their time," he would say to himself as he fended off invitations to bazaars, tea parties and women's clubs. When he had a free moment, he tried to do Zen meditation and yoga. The East seemed to have the only answer, for Christian prayer life had apparently dried up.

A discalced Carmelite told him that nobody read St. John of the Cross or St. Teresa of Avila anymore, not even Carmelites, and he hoped it was a false rumor.

Again he had a week's retreat with the Jesuits, and he told his spiritual director of his wordless prayer. "Read St. Teresa," his director said, crossing party lines, not caring who got the credit for this soul. For the first time, Paul plunged into the underground stream of the church's mystical tradition. As he prayed on that retreat, he had a vision in which the face of Christ became his own face. But when the retreat was over, he went back to his dry, busy life in the parish, and no longer saw the face of Christ.

"God, what have you done with my life?" Paul asked miserably one long Sunday night. "I would be better off without you." He was trying to decide whether or not to leave the next morning for the missions in Brazil. Probably priests in Brazil prayed no more than they prayed in America, Paul thought. "I've been running for my whole life," he told himself, "and never seem to get where I'm running to. Now I'm about to run all the way to Brazil, and what good will it do?"

Paul was right about the Brazilian missions. Early in his stay, a priest told him, "My work is my prayer." Translated, the priest's remark meant that he had made a choice about whether to say words or serve people. For this priest, as for so many, prayer was a formal duty, to be gotten out of the way as efficiently as possible so one could go about the real business of life. Paul didn't ask the priests in Brazil why they had trouble praying. To confront people was not his way. Instead, as he traveled on long bus rides through the bush, he boiled inside. The missionary priests might have been contemplatives, he thought, if only they had been shown how to pray. Many of them took solitary trips called "penetrations" deep into the interior for three days, going to small villages to listen to the troubles of the poor. Paul imagined himself sitting in the place of these priests, listening to problems he could not solve, seeing sickness he could not cure, and all the time with no interior life of his own, no nourishment. He was not strong enough, but would be one of the blind leading the blind, he thought. "Both of them falling into the ditch."

After six months he stopped short in the middle of his travels. He had been running, as always. Now he said flatly to himself, "There is no prayer life for a priest in this place. I can't help these people unless God is with me all the time. I'm not going to make it here." For two months more he waited, thinking he was selfish to leave. He loved the Brazilian poor people, suffering and beautiful in their simplicity. Someday when he had something to offer perhaps he would come back. But as of now he was as poor as they were.

In the past four years, Paul had packed his belongings 15 times. Almost everything he had given away—books, records, chalice. Moving so often had stripped him down. When he arrived at the Merton Center, having requested a 60-day retreat, Paul carried all he owned in one small suitcase. He certainly didn't bring his family's blessing with him. They had hoped he was coming home from Brazil to work in the local parish. After visiting briefly with them, Paul was oppressed by the noise of four television sets and people running in and out of the house at all hours. He prayed in the basement, even in the graveyard, searching as always for silence. He didn't have his order's blessing either, and didn't care. Institutions had not brought him any closer to God, and he was leaving them behind, as he had left his belongings. The Center had no baggage either; no thousand years of tradition weighed it down. Paul felt the farm was a new world, and he explored it as he had explored Brazil. This time he did not feel he had to search for God but that he was being found.

Often he sat in dryness looking at his brown and gold square on the chapel wall, but he understood now as he never had in the seminary that the dry times were when you absorbed the graces gained during the rich ones. Like a plucked string he oscillated between stillness and music. Sometimes he just sat; sometimes he saw a light deep within him that had circles around it, like the ripples left by a stone dropped in water. The life he was sharing at the Center was the one toward which he had felt pushed and drawn since the first disturbing days of seminary training, when he had learned that faith is not merely formal exercise, but a new way of being in the world, so that each moment is lived in the presence of God.

Now when he has finished his farm chores performed in prayer and silence, Paul sits for hours each day in the dimly lit Chapel of the Transfiguration. He no longer searches for the experience of God, for God happens to him from moment to moment, even when he rises in the cold Canadian dawn to make oatmeal for the community, then goes sleepily to the chapel, wishing he were back in bed. At such times he wonders what led him to this place where God is not a mere word, an idea neatly contained by rules and rituals, but an actual event, a drink of living water. When asked, he explains after a little pause, "I'm only at the beginning, but I think I know now what the contemplative life is. Instead of feeding words into silence, the contemplative waits for silence to grow into the word. That's what I wait for, too." He was silent for a little while, then smiled and said, "I might wait in Brazil. Now I think I could wait anywhere."

11 HEALING OF MEMORIES

> Out of his infinite glory, may he give you the
> power through his spirit for your hidden self
> to grow strong so that Christ may live in
> your hearts through faith, and then, planted
> in love, and built on love, you will with all
> the saints have strength to grasp the breadth
> and the length, the height and the depth, until
> knowing the love of Christ, which is beyond
> all knowledge, you are filled with the utter
> fullness of God.
>
> Ephesians 3:16-19

Like Father Paul, I was beginning to feel that all I did was wait. One of the things I waited for in the daily round of the Center's activities was the evening Mass. When we sat in our circle, faces to the chapel wall, I felt on my own. But when each night we heard the ancient words, said by Father Paul in his young voice, almost cracking in its newness, I woke up and felt ready for something to happen. No techniques were suggested on how to attend Mass. We just sat, our hands in our laps, and waited like young birds for their meal, our mouths open, ready to take all there was.

After Mass, we sat again, this time turned to face each other in the candlelight, sometimes looking at the sacrament exposed on the altar, sometimes not. Therese always knelt, her face lovely as a Russian icon, surrounded by soft gold, and Robert slumped into sleep, tired from his work and worry. Jane sat erect as a statue, determined to make the hour count, while I fought sleep and distraction, glad to see the end of a day so full of work and self-slaying. If it weren't for the bad dreams, I would have longed to be asleep, but the chapel full of friends was a better place than my lonely bedroom, where I woke up and cried, not knowing whether or not I even wanted Martin anymore, not knowing what I wanted.

One night in the chapel the office phone rang in the distance, then feet sounded on the hardwood floors. Michael, who like an angel, was given the task of delivering messages, came to whisper in my ear that I was wanted and I left the chapel. Martin's voice came through to me over the wire, remote as an Englishman's and as cool. He wanted to know if I still loved him and asked as if inquiring whether or not a position had been filled. I still loved him and said so; the position could never be filled because he already had it. Martin had pretended that he was my doctor, afraid of being cut off by some spiritual iron curtain that lifted only in emergencies. For him this was an emergency since he didn't know what I knew, that he was loved. My own case was different. For me the emergency was always there. No doctor could patch me up. Martin had begun to seem like no more than a living memory, hanging far away at the back of my mind. What I had to learn was that memories are not really at the back of your mind but up front, where you must look through them in order to see the present.

The Healing of Memories every night after Mass was a special time in which I found myself whispering the word "yes" over and over. The no-saying was all gone, together with the world I'd left behind. All I could hang onto were Peter's words, "Remember your young years, and give away what went wrong. You don't want it anymore. You aren't going through this alone, so be glad. Christ is with you, healing all the sore spots as they happen. Think of him beside you."

We worked on our past, year by year, over the month at the Center, starting at the present and working back. Linda wisely had us do this painful self-surgery before the Blessed Sacrament, which visually reminded us of the loving presence of Christ. We asked to have our minds opened so that we could see the forgotten but still raw wounds and be ready to forgive those who had hurt us. As we struggled through the years of our lives, we would certainly trip over our sins, but our guilt was to be dealt with during the sacrament of reconciliation, not here.

We were not concerned with finding out whether anyone had hurt us deliberately or not, but only with the healing of the wound itself. Our own power would not be enough to do that, I knew, because all my life I had tried to forgive my father for not loving me as much as he loved himself. Now I concentrated on Linda's way, asking Christ to heal the one who wounded me, as Jesus himself had asked his Father to have mercy on those who killed him: "Father, forgive them, for they know not what they do." In some mysterious manner, the forgiveness was to come through us. Not only would God heal the one who hurt us, but he would make us the instrument of that healing. We would take an active part in the work. As I thought of my father's aging face with its haunted, terrified eyes, it seemed to me that I was seeing my own. And as I forgave him and ceased to blame him for what I was, I found that I was forgiving myself.

A few months after my return from the Center, my father died suddenly. We had made our peace with each other. After the funeral, his older sister told me that their mother had beaten him every night with a horsewhip because he couldn't do his mathematics. He too had much to forgive.

The Healing of Memories was a lonely time for most of us, especially for the quiet French Canadian nun who never made a mistake but felt no joy in her goodness. Anna had waited almost half a century for joy and was about to give up hope.

12 THE STORY OF ANNA

See, I am doing a new deed,
even now it comes to light;
can you not see it?
Yes, I am making a road in the wilderness,
paths in the wilds.
The people I have formed for myself
will sing my praises.
I it is, I it is, who must blot out everything
and not remember your sins.

Isaiah 43:19, 21, 25

As long as Sister Anna could remember, she had felt alone. It had been too long, Anna thought, sitting on her chair watching the Blessed Sacrament which seemed to be floating over the altar in the evening dimness of the chapel. She ran one hand through her cropped, curly brown hair and held her full lips firmly together. Her trim, small form was straight in her chair, for Anna never slumped. Usually she didn't fidget either, but she was fidgeting a little now. How much longer could she go on? Anna asked herself, sure as she was that Jesus was only playing games with her. Hadn't he said he would love her if she loved him? Yet here she was, dried up like a starved plant, waiting to be watered by love, waiting, and still dry. All her life she had tried to love him, and now her heart was stone, as it had always been, except that stone was solid, hard to break whereas she felt brittle as plaster, empty and ready to crumble, with no one to catch the pieces. For a long time there had been no one. Now she was afraid even God didn't care what happened to her and her plaster heart. Had he ever cared? Was her whole vocation some big joke? It might well be, though as she looked back on her early years during the Healing of Memories, she wasn't sure if her life were a joke or a catastrophe.

Since her father's suicide and her stepmother's murder, she had wondered what in the world God had meant to prove by giving her the life she had lived or, rather, suffered. Other people would not have called it living. Or was all the sorrow a disguised blessing? If it were, Anna meant to know that blessing for what it was and thank God for it. She kept her eyes on the host, lying at the heart of the brass birdlike form on the shelf above the altar. "That I might be a bird," she said, sighing, "to fly away and be at rest." Never had there been rest for Anna and never in her childhood had there been love.

After their marriage, her French Canadian parents had left the city to settle on a small farm. Anna was their 13th child. Her mother had died shortly after this last child was born and from then on Anna was alone. Her father wanted to give her away for adoption to an aunt who was a drunk and whose own daughter, Anna's age, later died of alcoholism. Only the insistence of Anna's oldest sister Jeanne that the family not be separated saved Anna from being given away. Jeanne took care of the family as best she could, though four of the children died before their father married again.

His new wife was immature and mentally disturbed, unable to deal with nine growing children. Jeanne married and left the house because of the woman's intolerable presence. The other children lost any defense they might have had against the cruelty of their troubled stepmother. Anna stared at the host through the lens of tears, praying for the memories of that hard time to be healed. Even her father turned against her, becoming as crazy as his new young wife, and hitting his youngest child often. Once he struck her on the head with a pair of pliers. For years afterwards she feared her brain had been damaged by that blow. At last her father sent her away, perhaps realizing he could not give her the love she needed. She went to live with her sister Jeanne, whose children she was expected to mind. Jeanne was kind to her but preoccupied with her own responsibilities. The small children overwhelmed Jeanne, and she had no time left for Anna. Sometimes uncles and aunts visited and one spoke often to Anna of her dead mother, who had deeply loved the Lord. Whenever Anna asked Jeanne about their mother, wanting to know her better, Jeanne would begin to weep, so Anna learned never to speak about her loss or her need for love. Only by going from Jeanne's home to a girlfriend's did Anna know what it was to be loved. Her friend's family took her in as one of their own, and she went with them to movies and to church. The family she was born into had cast her out, she felt, and she had become an orphan.

Anna was only 13 when she left Jeanne's house for the city and a Catholic boarding school. During her first year at the school, her best friend disappeared. The girl had drowned herself in the river, and Anna was told by the nuns never to speak of her again. Someone who committed suicide was for the nuns a monster, to be shunned even in thought by pious people. Anna grieved guiltily and in secret, feeling her loss the more because this girl had been her only family as well as her only friend. The sisters did their best to reach the lonely girl, and soon the chores she did to earn her way at the school became not drudgery, but a way of showing the sisters that she loved them as they loved her. They taught her to serve the Lord and she gladly practiced what they taught. One of the nuns became her "little mother" and showed her how to share her life with Mary. In Mary, Anna found again the mother she had lost as a baby, and she served this mother with all her heart. In May of her last year at the school, Anna was given the privilege of crowning Mary queen, and during that same season she won first prize in a nationwide contest for an essay on the Marian year. Though the Mother of God was close to her, Jesus and the Father were as far away as ever.

When Anna was 15, her father killed himself, leaving her sad and astonished. Why hadn't he loved her, turned to her, shared with her the thoughts that drove him to take his life?

She would have listened, would have loved him. But he had not wanted her love, had given her away. Shortly afterward, her stepmother was murdered crazily in a local hotel. The lives of those who had been close to her seemed to her as random and meaningless as the shapes of clouds in a windy sky. She felt as if she stood on shifting ground and could be swallowed into it at any moment. Why did her father and her friend take their lives? Was their pain worse than hers? She could not believe it was. Yet she went on and on, smothering her sorrow, carrying the burden of it in her heart until it seemed to break. But no one was there to hear the sound of breaking or try to heal the fractures. She was alone, filled with shame and terror at the ugly violence of her family's history.

Did God care how alone she was? Anna wondered. If he cared, why didn't he lift her up, wipe her face, understand that she couldn't live anymore with this heavy, cold heart that hardly beat, hardly felt? She had lost too much and too often, she thought, tears beginning to roll down her cheeks. Candles lit the chapel dimly and the others could not see her cry. She could let the tears fall. Did God want her or not? She had prayed to Jesus and tried to love him, but he had remained silent, turning away his face from her. Now she was going directly to God the Father himself for help. If he would not take her up, then she would indeed be alone. For the first time she understood her father's despair, and endured his pain as her own. Would she end a suicide like him? Like her friend?

Anna put one hand over her heart, hoping it still worked, fearing it was altogether broken. She didn't want even to look at the picture of Jesus on the wall before her. He had promised to wipe the tears from her eyes, to make her a new creature, delivered from this body of death. All day she reminded him of that promise, saying her breath prayer over and over, "May your Spirit set me free." She had taped the prayer on her bedstead, on her desk, on her big brown leather Bible, on her place at the table, written it in indelible ink on her hand. Still, her spirit was a prisoner, left in its cage by Jesus, who didn't seem to want it. Perhaps the Father would take her into his own hands and not let her sit anymore in this awful stiffness, dryness, silence. She was afraid to cry out loud, afraid to disturb the others, but the tears kept coming like water struck from the rock by Moses. She was not praying, for she was too unhappy to pray. Prayer was a struggle, like everything else, and she was tired, too tired for any more struggling. She cleaned the bathrooms at the Center every day, serious as a martyr, determined to praise God at every breath, but all she got for it was heaviness, and no joy. Still Anna persisted, for if nothing else, her life had given her a rare persistence. As she peeled the potatoes she said her breath prayer, and as she scrubbed the shower curtains or the bathroom walls. Keep at it, she whispered grimly to herself, keep at it. God would see how she loved him and would love her in return. Certain words of scripture she read over and over, especially Revelation 3:20: "Behold I stand at the door and knock: if anyone hears my voice and opens the door, I will come in to him and will sup with him and he with me." When Anna looked for the door so she could open it, she remembered the Lord's words in John 10:9, "I am the door. Anyone who enters through me shall be saved and shall go in and out and find pasture." So Jesus was the door, Jesus himself, and it was Jesus she could not find. If he were knocking, she could not hear. She sat straighter in her chair, fixed her eyes on the picture of the Lord, willing him to let her hear his voice, his knock.

It was time to let go, Anna knew, her eyes filled with the whiteness of the host before her until she could see nothing else, time to forget what people might approve in her or not approve. She wanted to be with Christ, to sit gladly in his presence, at ease and loving, but her heart was hard and cold as stone. She remembered how he had left her to suffer alone, hadn't cared that her heart was broken. Yet now it was pounding as if it wanted to burst, and she put her hand over it again. Like the tears, this pounding was too much and might be noticed. She felt the dryness that had sucked up her convent years overcome her again. Even Jesus was rejecting her, just when she felt his closeness like living water in her mouth. Hadn't he said to knock at the door and it would be opened? But for her the door would not be opened. She was locked out.

The next day, Anna said her breath prayer with every breath she took even though the door had closed, leaving her outside. She would ask the Father, she thought, remembering with a chill in her cold heart the words of the Lord, "No one comes to the Father except by me." Well, she would go to the Father however she could.

For all her life the word "Father" had meant a balding, skinny man with the corners of his mouth turned down. Now the word "Father" mingled with the word "love," and meant something else to Anna. It meant day after day of sunlight, day after day of breaths taken, smiles traded back and forth with the sisters who had mothered her, the quick, sympathetic hugs of Brother Jonathan. Her poor, broken, earthly father was not all the God there was, nor the only source of love. God himself was the love she took into her body as she breathed, the food she prepared with her hands, the love of her sisters, the Eucharist she put in her mouth.

As she worked in the kitchen, carefully cutting the potatoes and onions into neat, tiny, pieces, she prayed over and over the new breath prayer she and Peter had chosen the night before: "Loving Father, be my love," and suddenly her heart thawed, moving in her with joy. She felt flowers open in her chest like roses in sunlight, sending shocks of life through her, until she leaned dizzily over the sink. It hurts to be this much alive she thought; it hurts to be this much loved. The Father was her Father. Her earthly father, sad and weak, had been only a shadow of the real one, not a source of love, but a poor man, to be pitied and forgiven. That night during the Healing of Memories she saw the Father's world like a garden and herself as a sacred, beautiful thing, growing in that garden, fed by the waters of love that flowed from the Father. Perhaps her love could free her father's crushed soul from the prison his suicide had sealed it in. The stepmother she had hated might also be freed if Anna could only love her, not with words and will, but with the love God was pulling out of her like breath and driven blood, a love not hers. As she prayed and forgave, her heart filled with a strange new passion for the people who had hurt her. She wanted to help them with a purity of intention one feels toward strangers. They had not hurt her; in their sorrow and pain they were nothing but her, nothing but the Lord. Before this moment, her heart had seemed to be stone, and she had forgiven only with her lips and with her will. Now she felt that the heart of Christ was beating in her, and that she loved these broken people with his own love.

A physical heaviness overwhelmed her that was nothing like the sleep she dropped into every night with such relief at the end of her nervous, driven days. She felt she was traveling deep into the dark tunnel that seemed to open in the center, between her eyes, gazing into the soul-lit icon, nothing in itself. Always she was tense, fearful, not ready to let go, because she was afraid no one would be there to catch her if she fell. But she was so tired of having to catch herself, so lonely and so tired with the effort of it.

The night before she had dreamed of being in a field of old, broken, discarded crosses. She gathered them up as if they were jewels, each one beautiful. In her heart she felt a deep, sudden longing to know God that was so strong it made her shake like a tree in the wind. Light seemed to fill her and she felt transparent, shining from inside like the icon in front of her. She herself was the icon, the door. The wave of clean water in her rose. Standing poor and naked, small before God, Anna was very glad. She listened to her own breathing and appreciated it, thinking it was Christ's, not hers, as it came and went inside her. The Father had not forgotten after all. This time she was remembered, loved. He had given her his Son. Anna felt herself carried in God's hands like a precious object. Later that night she wrote in her journal, "When I began to have my life with the Father, it was a very different kind of world I seemed to be living in. It was his world and everything including myself was seen as something very beautiful and sacred. I wanted never to make it ugly, and to stay close to the Father. Never again would I doubt his love." The grief of the past had melted away like dew at sunrise. Perhaps those who had hurt her were still suffering for what they had done; she wanted to release them as she had been released, let in through the door. "Forgive," she said with only her lips moving, thinking of her father. "Forgive," and felt the hatred for her crazy, dead stepmother fall away like leaves from a tree. "Nothing but love," she whispered, surprised and glad. "Nothing is left but love."

Soon after Anna's healing, we heard a tape by Sister Margaret Dorgan on St. John of the Cross. She explained the reason for our tears during deep prayer: we feel, she said, not so much sin and remorse as a growing closeness to God. The better we know his goodness, the less good we know ourselves to be. Catherine de Vinck wrote of God, "He is that light to which the sun is shade." If we see darkness when we look through ourselves at him, it's because we don't really want to see light and rub our eyes when the light turns on. St. John of the Cross explained why I was in darkness, but no one seemed able to explain how I could get out of it. The healing was becoming unbearably painful, the darkness too deep, and I asked God to end it, at least to end the bad dreams. That night I had my last one. Fat Brother Jonathan and fragile old Michael, who did more work than any of us despite his history of heart attacks, were at the seashore with me, and we were being flooded out of our house by a tidal wave. The men carried my bag, which had grown too heavy for me to lift, up a tall marble staircase. At the top we saw in the distance a new world, full of rounded glass domes, glowing with light, promising good things.

When Linda read this entry in my journal, she sent me out for a holiday, sure that I was ready to crack up. Probably she was right. The bag was really heavier than I could bear. "See the neighborhood sculptor," she said, remembering my love for making statues of clay. "But watch out. He's a lady's man."

Though since Martin came into my life I knew better, my old self still hoped to find a romantic soul mate who would sweep me off my feet into some cinematic cloud-cuckooland. This sculptor sounded like an answer to the wrong kind of prayer, and I hoped he would not be at home.

Old Michael, always quick to serve, drove me to the sculptor's ramshackle studio, which was surrounded by heaps of automotive junk and broken furniture. A fancy station wagon sat in his driveway, looking as out of place as a mink coat at a flea market. Clearly one of the ladies had arrived. We knocked on the sculptor's door. After a while he came out, wearing a robe, with his legs bare. He was busy, he said, when I asked if I might spend some time with him. He scratched his head of thick black hair and shuffled his feet. We stood looking at each other, wondering what to do next, until abruptly the artist turned around and closed the door in our faces.

So much for my notions of romantic love with a bohemian, some phantom soul mate who would make my life into a grade-B movie. During the trip with Michael I had idly daydreamed that the sculptor and I would fall into each other's arms. Now I saw that this hairy-legged artist, seizing a furtive hour with some bored housewife, was just a poor creature like myself, not knowing where to put his love. Only God could be loved, I knew at that moment, only God could be loved as I needed to love. No man was up to it. All the way home, Michael laughed, not offended at the way the world went because he was an old man who had seen what there was to see. As I sat back considering my lifelong failure as a heroine of song and story, I laughed a bit too.

Back at the Center, still enjoying my day off, I wandered into the back yard. In the past, I had gone to sit inside the fence, where I liked to swing, but today the area had been hastily, and to my mind rather ungenerously, marked "private" by a scribbled-on sheet of paper. No one else ever came to the fenced yard with the porch swing, so this sign meant me. My occasional trespassing had been noticed, it seemed. Turf is always private, I thought. Even here, the territorial imperative is in effect.

Ignoring the sign, I went through the gate and sat on a rock by a little duck pond, swatting mosquitoes when they became too insistent. Sounds echoed from the chapel and I supposed that the others were reading the scripture before the sunset session of wordless prayer. At that moment, the chapel didn't seem the place for me. I was busy being a trespasser.

The retreat was drawing to an end and yet I was still hanging onto my old life, just as I had hung onto the notion that the lady-killing sculptor might be an answer to prayer. Despite the silence and the aloneness, I had kept thinking that someone else could solve my problem, take care of me, put me back together, like one of the broken things Martin wanted to fix. Perhaps what I really wanted was to be in the arms of a parent, lover, friend. Nobody was available that day, only the warm wind, the birds, and the mosquitoes, which was just as well. The last thing I needed at that moment was an easy way out.

When I thought about what I expected of Martin, of the retreat, of Christ, I was suddenly embarrassed, like somebody who had thrown her garbage in the street and was about to be apprehended by the authorities. What I wanted was God and the world too, every kind of love I could get. Like Brother Jonathan with his food or Robert with his sex, I couldn't give up my toys. The sight of the sculptor came back to me, as he closed his heavy door no doubt to hurry back to his visiting housewife. He too was a trespasser, an overgrown child looking for a toy. All of us had come to the Center to learn how to put away our toys, to put away everything but God.

Thinking of the sculptor and his lady of the station wagon, I laughed, and settled on the rock next to the duck pond, not wanting the swing after all. Like the sculptor, I had trespassed, and then didn't want what I had found. No more toys for me, I decided, no more hairy sculptors, just whatever God made available of himself in the moment he gave me. Looking around as I sat on the rock, I was suddenly aware that for the first time in all my memory, I didn't want anything. The long days of silence, of the breath prayer, of the concentration on a single point were doing their work, though I didn't think of that until afterwards, so caught up was I in the hardness of the rock and the sweetness of the air. A duck flew down, waved his wings, stood on the water and danced, in an act of faith, falling into an unfamiliar element, not minding. As he plunged under the surface, the very air around me and the rock seemed to drop away, and for some time I too was in an unfamiliar element, by an act of faith. In my journal I wrote a description of what I felt before and after that time, however long it was, when nothing was happening at all, except that I was held up in loving arms, very much at rest. Of those moments themselves I have no description.

> I sat on a flat rock from where you could see the mountain, split by the crooked pine tree in front of me. Both were doubled in the dark water. It seemed as if I sat still on that rock only about ten minutes, but apparently over an hour had passed. By the time I got back, the others had finished dinner.
>
> No visions came to me on the rock, just a long time between the intake and the outgoing of breath, a total absorption in all that was spreading around me, a sense that

it was in motion, each moving thing making its own sound, whether or not I could hear it.

The first time I was born it was into an alien world, one I never got to like or feel at home in, but this birth was a different story. After sitting a while, I discovered that the spindly young pine tree only *seemed* crooked when you looked at this curve or that. Taken as a whole, if looked at from base to topmost branch, it was perfectly straight. To me, during that time by the pond, it seemed nothing was crooked.

The sun went down. Still I sat, wrapped in stillness, wrapped in love, like an infant in strong arms. For the first time in my life love was not something I wanted or gave, but something I received into myself so entirely that I became what it was. The words of St. Paul were real to me: "I live, yet not I but Christ lives in me." This entry was the last in my journal. It seemed enough.

For others, though, a further step was possible. They experienced what Peter and Linda call "Heart to Heart" prayer. During our last week, we set up a picture of Jesus instead of our brown and gold square. At the center of it was a heart spreading rays outward. In our periods of wordless prayer, we were instructed to draw all our energies up into our hearts and exchange this very center of ourselves for the heart of Christ. We would then love not with our own love but with God's. We would love the universe as ourselves for we would contain it, be no different from it. In another tape on St. John of the Cross, Sister Margaret told us, "The whole universe is within you. You needn't go in pursuit of God. He is not outside yourself." All creatures, if we don't attach ourselves to them as an end, are theophanies, God-bearers, as St. Francis knew when he tamed "Brother Wolf" and spoke to the birds.

I can speak of the Heart to Heart prayer, the prayer of mystical union with God, only at second hand, for it never happened to me, perhaps because I was already as full as I could be at that time. St. Thérèse of Lisieux was told by her older sister how it is that one soul receives more than another, without God being unjust. After seating Thérèse at a table, Céline filled a large vase with water and then filled a thimble. "Which one is more full?" she asked the child. Thérèse now understood that full is full. No one wants to be more full than full.

So somebody else will have to speak for the Heart to Heart practice, and it should be Michael, the oldest of us, a man who had gone through the long, dark night described by St. John of the Cross. The Dark Night was not a punishment, Michael learned, but a quick way of adjusting weak human nature to a God beyond appetite, thought and image. During this time, a person feels like a failure and does a lot of crying. He feels not so much sinful as overwhelmed by the goodness of God. Michael cried more than most of us. He had just lost his wife and suffered three near-fatal heart attacks. If he were to see God in this life, it would have to be now or never. Michael had lived as a businessman in a world built for pleasure, not the joy Paul speaks of when he says, "I want you to be happy, always happy in the Lord; I repeat, what I want is your happiness. Let your tolerance be evident to everyone: the Lord is very near." Michael had spent a lifetime wondering why he couldn't touch the Lord, if the Lord were so near. That was why he had come to the Center. The rest of us used to watch him, wondering how it felt to be so old, so close to death, as he was. Michael would serve at Mass each day, his hands moving slowly as they laid out the simple pottery vessels on the wooden table that served us as an altar. The sunset always came at the same hour as our communion, and Michael's frail shadow cut through the scattered golden light on the polished floor, his silver hair glowing in what was left of the sun. His hands knew what to do and could do it even in sleep, because he had served at the altar for 60 years. It was the closest he had come to God, and he moved slowly because he wanted the closeness to last.

13 THE STORY OF MICHAEL

"I am the living bread which has
come down from heaven,
so that a man may eat it and not die.
Anyone who eats this bread will live forever.
And the bread that I shall give
is my flesh, for the life of the world."

John 6:51

From early in life, Michael had known that God was not
to be loved halfway. His mother, an Irish immigrant, knew
God as she did her husband and five children, as intimately as
air. From his mother Michael learned not to be content with
the remote God of the catechism.

His life was ordinary—years of schooling in business ad-
ministration, marriage and children, work in the world, service in his parish church. Throughout his life he had exercised
the theological virtue of hope. If he gave, he would be given
to. If he forgave, he would be forgiven. Michael hoped and
forgave, worked and served. But all the while he felt like a
machine that rumbled along a track, regular and unfeeling as
a train, stopping at all the places God wasn't to be found.

Michael grew tired of being a work machine and longed
to be something more, the hands of God in this world, the
breath of God breathed into the day's work. Something like a
priest, he wanted to be, but he would not have given up his
wife and children. At last, though, the children became their
own people, went away; his wife took a job and was busy
cooking and cleaning in the evenings. He felt choked by all
the love in him that could find no way out, and longed to
empty himself of it recklessly, like Mary Magdalene pouring
out her precious ointment on the feet of Christ, not caring
what it cost. The longing grew so intense that he began to

drink to dull it, for in his sober life he could express nothing of what he felt. Such feelings were not expected of a sensible businessman, and Michael was afraid to do the unexpected after so many years of being ordinary. Perhaps alcohol would deaden the longing, he thought, allowing him to live like other people, enjoying a lifetime of going through the approved motions.

Months and years went by, and he sank deeper into the glassfuls of peace, the ice tinkling cheerfully as his hands shook. Alcohol gave a rhythm to his day. At work he could look forward to the evening drinks that allowed him to walk through the day like a swimmer moving through water, slowly and with grace. When his family wanted him to seek help, he resented them, despite the gentleness of the urging. They wanted to keep him from the hazy, numbing world he entered alone every night. Michael told himself he wasn't bothering them. In fact, he had supported them all those years. Why wouldn't they let him be? The peace he sought seemed to be unattainable any other way. He knew because he had tried everything else. If God were unavailable, then he would settle for the sweet forgetfulness of drink.

Michael had forgotten that he was not alone, but surrounded by people who loved him. His brother sent a member of Alcoholics Anonymous to visit him. Michael eventually joined the organization, drawn by the friendliness of its members and their insistence on turning over their lives to God, or the Higher Power, as they called him. He became a member of AA, confessed regularly in group meetings that he was an alcoholic, and told his "drunkalog," the story of how he began drowning in alcohol, whenever he was asked to tell it. Hearing the stories of the others, telling his own, helping to rescue members who fell back into their old habits gave Michael a way of showing the love he had bottled up in himself after the children had gone their own ways.

Two honeymoon years went by in which Michael enjoyed daily Mass and experienced a closeness to God that was new to him. After a time, however, the ardor cooled, and he fell back on the secondary rewards of service at the altar and presence at a charismatic prayer group. It was a member of that group who gave him a copy of Linda's *Radiant Heart* (Dimension Books). Reading the book led him to decide on a retreat at the Center. Though he was told at first that he was only on the waiting list, he was sure Jesus meant him to be chosen, and he packed his bag.

Despite all his attempts at holiness, Michael's life was hollow and made hollow noises when he beat on it with his demands for love, joy or whatever music he had not heard after all these decades of straining his ears. How would he manage a whole month with nothing to do but pray? He wasn't sure. To go through a day without being upset was impossible for him. How could he manage a month of peace?

During his first day at the Center, the question was no longer in his mind. For a long time he had felt pain over his inability to know God directly, yet the light-touched hilltops ringing the valley and the swaying trees brought God's name to his mouth and made him present, familiar as one hand to the other. Never had he doubted in his mind that God was present, but only at long, separated moments had he been aware of God's closeness.

At first, his prayer in the chapel was scattered and awkward, like an adolescent's phone conversation with a stranger. As he said his breath prayer those first few days, he realized that he was talking to someone close, and he looked around from time to time, thinking to see whoever it was. The second day, according to his journal, Jesus was near. "This nearness wipes out my ambiguous statement yesterday about 'someone.' " Jesus was there. Before this time he had thought he was the one who initiated dialogue with God. Now he wasn't so sure.

One day as he sat in front of his gold circle, Michael gradually began to see a shrouded figure emerge, wave him on, then turn into a cross. After that, what he saw every day as he prayed before the circle was the crucifixion, while his own self died and died. The suffering face of Jesus spread its sorrow all over the gold circle, filling Michael's eyes and heart. Gradually he began to write in his journal of "my suffering Jesus," and wished he had been at the foot of the cross so that Jesus would not have suffered alone.

Communion had become a full meal to a hungry man. Offering the Eucharist to others was a joy to him. He liked holding out the cup to the mouths of the waiting communicants, and smiled up into their faces as he moved around the circle, feeling the goodness that came from them, tangible as a handclasp, feeling the generosity of God who had given him this cup. Michael became aware that Jesus had always been close, not a stranger, but that he himself had been absent. Holding the cup dark with wine, he was glad, giving God to his friends.

When Michael learned about the Consecration of Sexual Energies, he was astonished by its effect on his tired body. A geyser which he had drawn freehand and placed below his brown square on the wall seemed to be inside his body, rising upward, spreading a warm feeling into his chest and higher into his skull, tickling behind his ears. A tightness was in his throat and armpits; pins and needles prickled up and down his legs. He perspired freely, and suddenly his legs and feet seemed weightless, as though he were walking on the moon. His head leaned forward as if listening, for Jesus seemed to have something to say. He was not worried when the words were carried away as by a strong wind, knowing they would eventually be heard. Meanwhile his breath prayer, "Father, let me know your Son," had become more than words. On July 16 he wrote in his journal:

> This is something that happened about 9:15 last night when I was walking on the gravel road outside. Suddenly I noted that my breath prayer was not actually in my mind but was centered in the heart. My entire chest felt inflated.

Though he didn't know it at the time, this incident was the

beginning of Michael's experience with Heart to Heart prayer.

Peter introduced Heart to Heart prayer shortly after Michael had begun to feel the pressure rising in his chest. It was a relief to have the picture of Christ's radiating heart, for it moved him more than the gold circle. So hard did he work with the picture and the new prayer that he felt drained at the end of each day. After a journal entry mentioning his exhaustion, Peter, knowing how tired his heart was, wrote, "Please do take the rest you need, Michael." If Michael rested, he didn't say so in his journal. Probably he didn't, for he knew his time was short and felt the urge to work against the approaching night. The Eucharist filled him with strength and kept him going. Of the outdoor communion, when Toby and Philo played in the circle of people, Michael wrote that he felt the presence of God around him, warm as arms.

Looking at the picture of Christ's heart, Michael felt his own heart smothered and enveloped in radiance. The fullness of his chest spread through him and he breathed joy like air. The cleft of the geyser, where it split to spill on either side, seemed to cradle his fractured, tired heart. In his journal he wrote of this moment:

> Could feel the flow of energy pouring through the geyser into my heart and then outward to my shoulders and arms. Some sharp pressure was on the solar plexus until the energy pushed through to the heart. A great feeling of strength running throughout my body, my thighs, lower legs, chest, arms. Offered this flow of energy to Jesus afterward . . . complete relaxation. Even my head was bobbing like it was out of control.

The next morning Michael leaned into his Heart to Heart prayer like a runner against the ribbon at the end of a race. "A steady ache in my heart," he wrote in the journal. "Could feel its beating like surf in my ears . . .

Could visualize the radiance of Jesus' heart within, permeating my entire body. Heat in my chest and stomach. Intense ringing throughout my head. Radiance from the Sacred Heart seemed to cradle my heart, which felt like it was moving up and down in rhythm with the heart of Jesus. Whenever I looked at the picture, Jesus was smiling. It was good.

As his time at the Center came to an end, Michael knew better and better how good it was. The inside of his head seemed to be filled with light. He saw the passing of energy from Christ's heart to his own, quick as electric shocks, exquisite as a lover's fingertip. On July 26, two days before he left, he wrote:

During my adoration of the Sacred Heart, I looked directly into the picture of Christ. A sudden burst of power into my heart, spreading all over my body, down to my toes. I know that it came from Jesus' heart to mine. May be presumptuous, but I believe it was pure love. Magnificent feeling of Jesus within me. The whole room filled with his holy essence. My heart dancing within me in the radiant light of the Sacred Heart. Then it seemed like my heart was ablaze and burned by the fire of Christ's. There is no God but my God and there never shall be. Who could be so generous? Thank you, Father.

Michael went to the hermitage with some fears. He was a sociable man, not used to being alone. Yet he longed to be intimate with God. On entering the bare little shack in the woods behind the farmhouse, he wrote: "I invite the Father, Son and Holy Spirit to reside with me." He sat in a hard chair beside the window, facing the mountain, the sun in his eyes until he closed them. From the journal:

Steady ache deep in my chest, my heart longing to be consumed by Jesus' heart. . . . A definite, intense experience of Jesus' presence within me was apparent. Later I became aware of what I believe was the presence within me of the Triune God. At first a shivering sensation pervaded my entire body. I was a little frightened. When it dawned on me that at that time I had become the home of the Father, Son and Holy Spirit, I was overjoyed. For me this hermitage was holy ground.

The stay in the hermitage was for Michael the most significant time he spent at the Center. All his life had led him to this moment.

At last I felt I had a personal God. One thing I know: until my life is finished, resting with Jesus, I haven't made it.

This retreat is my last one. It will not be over until I die.

14 OUT OF THE CENTER

As for me, my life is already being poured
out as a libation, and the time has come for
me to be gone. I have fought the good fight; I
have kept the faith.

2 Timothy 4:6-7

We had all been running hard, and our blood was up.
Now it seemed nothing could break our stride and we were
full of hope. No desire was left in us to eat up the world. Of
course we wanted to stay on and on at the Center. Some did,
but most of us had to prepare for the next step, remembering
that when people were hungry, they had Jesus' promise to
feed them.

Linda and Peter called us together for a last session
before we left, giving us sober warnings. "Don't be anxious to
become a saint overnight," Linda said. "It's hard going and
happens in God's own time. Over the months, repeat your
Healing of Memories. You're pregnant and fragile, bearing
the new life of Christ within you. Don't let any poison touch
that life. The old patterns will try to take over, the old fears
will come back sometimes, but you know what happened to
you here and you won't forget. In time you may wonder
whether or not it really happened. Don't be fooled. It happened." Linda paused longer and longer between sentences.
"Your friends will wonder about you. Let them." When she
sat down, Peter opened his Bible and read St. Paul's goodbye
to the Philippians:

There is no need to worry; but if there is anything you
need, pray for it, asking God for it with prayer and
thanksgiving, and that peace of God, which is so much
greater than we can understand, will guard your hearts and
your thoughts in Christ Jesus. Finally brothers, fill your
minds with everything that is true, everything that is noble,

149

everything that is good and pure, everything that we love
and honor, and everything that can be thought virtuous or
worthy of praise. . . . Then the God of peace will be with
you.

They both made the sign of the cross, were silent a-
while, and sent us away.

And so I went home to Martin, to a life that was what I
once thought I wanted. Martin met me at the airport, looking
awkward, not knowing what to expect from a person who
had been living in silence for a month. He supposed I had
become weird, stricken with some Christian mania, and had
grown away from him altogether. What I saw in him now,
and couldn't tell him, was another self, not divided from me,
but as tender, vulnerable and lovable as a new infant. When I
saw him waiting at the terminal gate, his cowlick standing
straight up, uncombed and forgotten, his face uncertain,
hopeful, I understood what Grace, the black landlady, had
felt for my little son. This man was to be loved because he
was a lamb of God, not because he had something to offer
me, not because I was in need. He was to be loved for just
what he was.

"Well, where are we now?" Martin asked as he drove me
home. "In the same place?"

"It's never the same place," I said, thinking of how St.
Thérèse had said, "Once I love, I love forever." Martin was
one of those I would love forever, whether or not we saw
each other again. In my absence, he had changed none of his
ideas about the world, but was surer than ever that we should
take all we can from it, be comfortable here and now, giving
no thought to outworn moral codes or mystical notions. I
was back home all right, in the real world again, and the
Center seemed dim and far away.

As we spoke late into that homecoming night, I saw the
long bad dream of his childhood and the longer one of
solitary manhood crushing out of him any trust in a God who
loved his children. Nobody in Martin's world loved anyone,

except to gain an advantage by it. For him, marriage was a
dead institution, one that bound a man against his best interests to a woman who demanded security as a payoff for
sex. A temporary living together was the only arrangement
that Martin felt was honest. A woman who really loved a
man, he argued, would not ask him to give up his freedom,
his separateness, his individual self. And of course that was
precisely what he would have to give up, just as the lover of
God has to give up the illusion that he runs his own life, and
acknowledge that he is only a cell in the tissue of the world,
married to the whole body by solemn contract, by a gift of
the heart. "The husband is the wife's and the wife is the husband's," Jesus said, loving his church as a man loves his
bride, as a vine loves its branches.

Martin's heart drew him to a vision of a world run by
love, as it drew him to me, but his head insisted on a life of its
own, not acknowledging dependence on any other being. It
was a dignified, sad posture, which I respected but could not
share. So we agreed to go our own ways. I cried a lot that
night, not wanting to let go, not wanting to lose this man,
and Martin ended by holding me close to him.

"*Lay keppi*," he said, in his mother's Yiddish, putting my
head on his shoulder before going away. "*Lay keppi*." If there
is any more to give up than Martin, I don't want to know
what it is.

Because I was determined to be like Linda and give up
what might stand between God and me, I put my rambling
lakeside house in New Jersey up for sale and went to live in
the Bronx, where I thought I would be uncomfortable and
useful. "There is no sacrifice if you're in love," Linda had
said, and I found her words to be true. My one room in the
city was quite enough for me, and I was not uncomfortable at
all. Probably I was not very useful either, for I found new
distractions to take up my time as soon as I rid myself of the
old ones, like the householder in the gospels who cleaned out
seven devils and was invaded by seven more. God had said,

"I will have mercy, not sacrifice," and I began to think I had gotten the message backwards. Lots of sacrifice, but little mercy, little love. Clearly, living the contemplative life when all alone is dangerous business, as Linda had warned us before we left. If we are alone, there is no one to practice loving on except ourselves.

I found myself missing Martin very much, as I missed the Center. In his straight talk as in Linda's, I had heard the truth about my own notions, my compulsive need for love. When I had wanted love, Martin had demanded that I give it. When I had wanted fathering, Martin let me know I was indulging myself, though he hugged me even as he told the truth. Now, without him, I felt undirected. No one was there to tell me when I was being selfish. Before, Martin's hurt and anger had held up a mirror to my bad temper, just as his pleasure in being loved had taught me the pleasure of loving. Perhaps I could not have loved God, unless Martin had been given to me first. Perhaps we were both being taught how to love, so that someday we would be able to love God.

Suddenly I saw clearly why Martin and I had been given to each other. God was not cheated by my loving him through Martin, and he gave Martin assurance of his love through me. God was the one giving and receiving love, whatever the source, whatever the object. When Martin and I had comforted each other, healed our mutual memories, wiped the tears from our eyes, we were not ourselves only, but God loving in us. I had always believed that God could not bear to share me with anyone, attributing my own weaknesses to him, and that was why I had given Martin up. Yet if the retreat had taught me anything, it had taught me that God was the beginning and end of love, and that when the least of our brothers was held in our arms, we held him.

I wanted to call Martin to tell him so, but he had rented his house and gone away. Some friends said that he was studying with a spiritual healer, but they had no idea where, having been too surprised to ask. I remembered Martin's love for fixing what was broken, and how much he had helped to fix me. I prayed for him, putting him in God's hands, though I knew he was already there. Martin seemed lost to me, and I had to give him up all over again. This time it wasn't so hard, because I had learned at the Center that I was not supposed to play God in anyone's life. Still, as the last leaves fell, and the first snowflakes, I asked God often to be with my friend and with me.

EPILOGUE—THE LAST RETREATANT

A time went by, and then Martin wrote, saying he wanted to see me again and talk about some odd experiences that were changing his life.

"What happened with this spiritual healer?" I asked him as we sat in a Chinese restaurant, sharing the house dinner. "Nothing much happened to me, even at the Center. Only a little thing by the pond, watching the ducks." I wanted to let him off the hook, in case nothing big had happened to him either.

Martin stirred his tea, though he hadn't put anything in it. "You aren't the only one trying to find a way to live," he said. "Sometimes the way isn't clear. I heard when you told me what happened to you, even though you thought I didn't. Actually I went back to the synagogue, my first Yom Kippur in 25 years. I cried some, hearing the Hebrew again."

"You have something to tell?" I was afraid of Martin's face, stern and remote as an angel's. "You don't have to."

"I thought I'd try praying," Martin said, pushing his food aside. "Never had before, but why not? So I did." He laughed silently, turning his palms up. "I just sat still, the way you were doing, only I went on a retreat with an Orthodox rabbi. While I was sitting still, I saw some things." Martin stopped abruptly and began to eat again, not seeming to want the food as much as not to go on talking.

"What did you see?" I asked, feeling a bit jealous. As on the retreat, everyone seemed to see interesting things except me. Linda said not to worry that my prayer was ordinary, but still, I wished I had seen something worth telling.

"It was like being hit on the head and seeing light," he said, "I saw Moses, and beside him, would you believe, Christ. So much light around them, like two wheels spinning in my eyes." He shook his head. "How would you feel if you saw that? What would you do with yourself?"

"How did you know it was Christ?" I asked, aware that Martin had been raised as an Orthodox Jew with no Christian archetypes in his unconscious. "Moses, maybe, but Christ you never heard of. How come he turned up in your prayer?"

"I knew who it was," Martin said, breaking his fortune cookie noisily into pieces. "Afterward it wasn't hard for me to believe in God. I wasn't sure what to do about believing, but helping people seemed like a good thing. That's when I started visiting hospitals with this rabbi, the one who gave the retreat. He prayed for the patients and touched them, so I started doing it too. When I put my hands on sick people, they felt better and so did I. But I'm not religious. I only wanted to help, if I could."

Martin explained to me that when we had gone our own ways, he had suddenly felt a need to put aside what divided him from other people, and to touch them until they knew they were loved and well. He did not know where the longing came from, but was sure it was the same love that he had always wanted for himself. In touching hurt, broken bodies, he had found himself loving, and had wanted to pray. "I feel open as a door," Martin said, tearing up his paper fortune. "With everything going through. Herds of elephants. Whole galaxies. All there is. Loving seems very good to me."

About that time, Peter and Linda stopped in New York to see me, and Martin came to see them. He wound up alone with Peter, talking about how it was to be raised in a Jewish family. Later Peter told me that Martin was very holy and that he loved my friend very much. The two of them had talked late that night they met, though I never knew what they said.

Over the next year I stayed in touch with Martin as he turned away from his old life, putting his fear of other people behind him and learning how to help those who had suffered as he had.

"I don't know how I do it," he told me. "I forget." He really did forget, because he lived only in the moment, the way Linda had taught us how to live. "I'm no healer, no more than anyone else. Just a door that the healing goes through. An antenna."

Linda and Peter kept Martin's picture on their desk and prayed for him, as if he had been on retreat like the rest of us. In a way, Martin had been in a hermitage of his own, eating white Benedictine cheese and brown bread, loving God under the soles of his feet, in the open palms of his hands, like the singing monks, not setting any rules for where he would love or not love.

He tried to explain to me over the long-distance wire from California, when I asked if he thought he was being converted. "No, I'm not an organized Christian," he said, reminding me that he was, as always, his own man. "But neither was Jesus, after all. He was a Jew and a healer. That sounds right to me, and enough. I feel like I'm on retreat all the time, like there's nothing left of me. Is that how you felt at the Center?" His voice faded and came back strong. "Anyway, that's how I feel."

As for me, at the other end of the vanishing connection, I felt embarrassed that I had not really expected prayers to be answered. "Linda says you belong in the story," I called out, hating to hear his voice go away. "She says you were part of it. Should I put you in? Would you mind?"

He came back to New York to talk about it.

"You can tell what's happened to me," he said. "Don't say you know where I'm going. I don't know myself. But I think we're all at the center, whether we know it or not." He stood at the window of my Bronx apartment, the sun turning his hair bright, and without looking at me, he reached behind him and took my hand.